THE RETURN OF THE
VIKINGS
THE BATTLE OF MALDON 991

THE ANGLO-SAXONS

A SERIES OF ACCESSIBLE HISTORIES OF KEY ASPECTS OF ANGLO-SAXON ENGLAND.

SERIES EDITOR
Donald Scragg, Emeritus Professor of Anglo-Saxon Studies at the University of Manchester

PUBLISHED
Donald Scragg, The Return of the Vikings: The Battle of Maldon 991

FORTHCOMING
Ian Howard, Harthcanute: Last Danish King of England

FURTHER TITLES ARE IN PREPARATION
Athelstan: England's First King
Edward the Confessor
Harold I Harefoot
Edmund Ironside
Edward the Elder
Offa
The Conversion of Britain
St Bede
The Kingdom of Mercia
The Kingdom of Wessex: A History of the West Saxons
The Kingdom of East Anglia: A History of the East Angles
The Kingdom of Essex: A History of the East Saxons
The Kingdom of Sussex: A History of the South Saxons
The Kingdom of Northumbria: A History of the Northumbrians
The Kingdom of Kent: A History of the People of Kent
The Viking Wars 793-1080
Anglo-Saxon England: A Historical Companion
Anglo-Saxon Churches: A History
The Anglo-Saxon Chronicle
The Germanic Invasion of England: Angles, Jutes, & Saxons
Pagans: Paganism in Anglo-Saxon England

THE RETURN OF THE
VIKINGS
THE BATTLE OF MALDON 991

DONALD SCRAGG

TEMPUS

First published 2006

Tempus Publishing Limited
The Mill, Brimscombe Port,
Stroud, Gloucestershire, GL5 2QG
www.tempus-publishing.com

British Library Cataloguing in Publication Data.
A catalogue record for this book is available from the British Library.

ISBN 0 7524 2833 0

Typesetting and origination by Tempus Publishing Limited
Printed in Great Britain

Contents

About the Author

Donald Scragg is Emeritus Professor of Anglo-Saxon Studies at the University of Manchester. He is the author of *A History of English Spelling*, editor of the standard edition of *The Battle of Maldon* poem, editor of a series of essays in *Battle of Maldon AD 991*, and co-editor of *The Blackwell Encyclopedia of Anglo-Saxon England*. He lives in Manchester.

Acknowledgements

I am grateful to many friends and institutions for allowing me to reproduce their illustrations, in particular to Simon Keynes and Mark Blackburn. All are acknowledged individually in the captions to the plates. Rikke Johansen of the Vikingship Museum at Roskilde deserves special mention for overcoming the difficulties of electronic transmission, and I am particularly indebted to Gill Cannell, sub-librarian of the Parker Library, Corpus Christi College, Cambridge, and Cressida Annesley, Acting Archivist of Canterbury Cathedral, for facilitating permissions. Basil Blackwell Ltd graciously agreed that I should use material from my earlier book on the battle of Maldon. Finally, Jonathan Reeve of Tempus Publishing was consistently supportive and very patient during the overlong gestation period of this book.

Prologue

It was early August in 991. The millennium was approaching and many superstitious men feared its coming, expecting that it would bring the end of the world, but in the village of Sturmer on the northern border of Essex, Leofson was untroubled. It was a warm Sunday and he sat outside with a few friends, tenant farmers like himself, contemplating his lot. He found that it was good. He had a wife and young family, and was well able to keep them in comfort. The forest which pressed in upon the village on all sides offered good wood for building and fires, as well as mast for his two dozen pigs. His sheep had bred well that year, nearly eighty of them now, and that meant that his dairymen had provided a fine supply of cheese for the winter with the salt he had bought from Maldon, and during the summer his flock had supplied him with a heavy weight of wool for which he had got a good price from the Ipswich merchant who regularly bought from him. Like most of the farmers he knew, he kept few cattle, just enough to provide him with the team of oxen which were amongst his most precious possessions. The eight oxen which he was working at the moment were strong enough to cultivate all of his land without his having to use his slaves to pull a hand-plough, as many of his fellow-farmers, smallholders who were less fortunate than himself, had to do. This meant that even in spring two of his four slaves could be released for other duties as only two were needed for the ploughing. One was an excellent bee-keeper, his three hives working the forest so successfully that the whole household had honey for sweetening and preservative all winter. As long as he could remember, the farm had had a surplus, which he took to market down in Maldon or Colchester. He preferred Maldon. Colchester was too large, too noisy, for a man used to the quiet of the countryside as he was. It would be time to take some pigs soon and perhaps the male calf that was born last spring, now well grown and needing to be killed before the winter came when the fodder in the hay-barn must be reserved for his newly expanded flock of sheep. His doves too had bred well this year, and there would be good eating to be had from them in the spring when other meat was exhausted, though he himself preferred rook pie to one made from pigeon meat. He had a man who was adept at bringing down with his slingshot the birds that were in the large rookery at the edge of the wood, where the numbers would expand significantly with the early spring hatchings, supplying many tender young rooks for cooking. Yes, he would sell as many of the doves as he could.

Best of all, he thought, as his mind revolved around his good fortune, his land was productive, and he was well served by his lord. He leased the twenty acres of his manor from Byrhtnoth, the ruler of Essex, who was a just and honourable man and had been a good friend to him. In turn, he offered without question the services which he was bound to as a tenant, riding duties occasionally and, in time of need, service in the army on behalf of the village. The latter need had never arisen in his lifetime. The old king had ruled the land with a firm hand, so firm that no foreign man had dared to invade as they had in the time of his predecessors. Since his day – it must be sixteen years ago now since his death – there were rumours of difficulties far away in Wessex, but Lord Byrhtnoth had maintained order in Essex and Cambridgeshire, and he had heard of no problems in nearby Suffolk. No, he counted himself fortunate. Last week the villagers had celebrated Lammas, the harvest festival, in the little stone chapel that he could see across the meadow, and harvest was in all of their minds as they prepared to cut the hay. But it was the lake that they had been talking of just then, the huge lake near the village, the source of the River Stour, which was a rich source of fish and eels all year round and which would be full of ducks and geese, bitterns and rails, woodcock and snipe next month to add to the partridges in the forest in providing excellent hunting. Yes, he thought, his life was good.

Suddenly he was on his feet, his reverie broken. Everyone around him was up too, straining to hear more sounds of an approaching rider. They had all heard the trumpet blast which heralded his coming from afar. When he galloped into sight, his horse foaming with the effort of a long ride at speed, he made straight for Leofson, whom he recognised from their training days. Pausing only to pant out his message, that there was a general call to arms, and that Leofson was to ride to Colchester fully armed immediately because, it seemed, the Danes were invading the country and had already sacked Ipswich, he dug in his heels and rode on north towards the next village of Kedington. Leofson quickly called instructions for his brown cob to be saddled while he went to dress for his journey. The crowd scattered, only to reassemble shortly afterwards in greater numbers to watch him embrace his wife and children and mount his horse. He was dressed now in a thick woollen tunic

and tight stockings, despite the warm weather, with black
leather ankle boots, and had stuck a long knife into his
girdle. He had dispensed with the cloak that he normally
wore for riding. As he sat in the saddle behind the bundle of
throwing spears that were strapped across its front, his serv-
ants passed up his long spears which he held upright in his
right hand, before Godric, the slave who had been with his
family longest, lifted up with an effort his heavy, wide, round
shield of wood covered with oxhide and bound with a thick
metal rim. Leofson slid his left arm through the metal ring
behind the heavy central boss, and lifted it in salute to the
freemen and women, villagers and slaves, who stood around
him. He called out with a steady voice, 'My friends, I vow
that when you see me again, you will have no cause to taunt
me that I fled one foot's length from the struggle and came
home without honour. I will avenge my countrymen in
battle, or else spear and sword will take me.'

To a roar of encouragement from the village which
drowned out the sounds of weeping of those dear to him
which he did not want to hear, Leofson clapped his heels
to his mount abruptly and, with his blood racing, rode off
to war.

I

Pillage and Settlement

Viking attacks on England began two centuries earlier than 991, long before England existed as a single
political unit. Early Anglo-Saxon England consisted
of many independent kingdoms. Gradually the smaller were
absorbed by the larger, until by the beginning of the ninth
century, the land was divided into four: Northumbria, East
Anglia, Mercia and Wessex (see Map 59). The relative power
of these kingdoms lay largely in the strength of their indi-

vidual kings. As one king grew in strength, others became weaker and had to wait for the death of their rival in order to regain some of the power enjoyed by their predecessors. Nonetheless, these four had survived for many generations and retained a good part of their independence from one another when the ninth century began in 800. The largest in area was Northumbria, consisting of all the lands north of a line stretching from the Humber estuary in the east to the Mersey in the west and extending as far as modern Edinburgh. South of the Humber, the dominant kingdom at the very beginning of the ninth century was Mercia, covering the whole of the midlands. Whereas at an earlier period both East Anglia and Northumbria had had their turns of over-lordship of the south-humbrian kingdoms, during the eighth century Mercia had grown in strength, subjugating earlier, smaller adjoining kingdoms like Essex, and gaining major influence in East Anglia and Wessex as well. In the first quarter of the ninth century, it was the turn of Wessex to dominate. Having begun as a relatively small kingdom south of the Thames, it first absorbed Kent and the Celtic areas of Devon and Cornwall, and then extended its influence north of its traditional border of the Thames to Wales and Mercia. Wessex was thus the last of the great kingdoms of the country to achieve prominence in England as a whole, but its domination was ultimately to prove the most enduring.

The story of the rise of Wessex is intimately tied to the first wave of Viking attacks against English shores, yet the most infamous of those early attacks was not against Wessex itself but against the eastern seaboard of Northumbria. Small groups of Vikings began raiding lightly defended settlements on the coast of England at the close of the eighth century, and the most poorly guarded settlements of all, as well as potentially the most rewarding in terms of the treasure they contained, were monasteries. What the church saw as the most barbarous act of Viking aggression was the sack in 793 of the celebrated monastery of Lindisfarne, now Holy Island, near Berwick-on Tweed. Lindisfarne had been founded in the early years of English Christendom in the late sixth century and was venerated later as the seventh-century home of St Cuthbert who died in 687. Thanks to the writings of churchmen, the effects of this attack reverberated through Christian Europe, and quickly became the symbol of Viking barbarism. An equally significant raid in the following year involved another north-eastern monastery, usually assumed to be Jarrow, home of Bede until his death in 735, while the *Anglo-Saxon Chronicle*, which in its early years was written entirely from the point of view of Wessex, records the first attack by the Vikings on English shores under the annal for 789 when three ships from Norway attacked Portland in Dorset and killed the king's reeve. Although this date appears to contradict the tradition that the Lindisfarne raid signalled the start of major Viking attacks, the precise year of the Dorset raid is uncertain. It occurs in the *Chronicle* in conjunction with a note on the marriage of King Brihtric to the daughter of King Offa of Mercia in 789 and is the only *Chronicle* reference to Brihtric who ruled Wessex from 786 to 802. The chronicler simply notes that the Dorset attack took place during Brihtric's reign, and his evidence may not be reliable since the *Chronicle* was probably not compiled until the end of the ninth century when precise details of the attack had been forgotten. Although all these raids were no more than isolated incidents in themselves, they were the start of a pattern of incursions by marauding Vikings across northern Europe during this period. In 795, Vikings who had established a base in the Shetlands sailed round to the western side of Scotland and attacked Iona, another significant monastic site, while from the end of the century, attacks from Scandinavia along the northern coast of mainland Europe, particularly on the Low Countries, then part of the extensive Franco-German empire, became so numerous that the emperor Charlemagne established a regular coastguard to police his realm.

Reports of Vikings in Christian writings from the period almost exclusively concern their raids, raids which initially were driven by mixed motives, and certainly developed, in part, out of commercial expeditions. Given the nature of the settled lands along the coastlines in Scandinavia, the inhabitants were adept seamen, and consequently for a time were the greatest traders of Europe. The *Chronicle* report of 789 notes that the Dorset reeve had gone initially to the Viking ships to take the sailors to the king to impose the appropriate taxes on them, assuming that they were traders. Lawful trading by Vikings, in fact, continued throughout the ninth century, and this trading was with England as well as with the rest of Europe. There were Viking traders at the court of King Alfred at the end of the ninth century, even during the period when the country was harried with renewed Viking invasions. In the early period it was probably difficult on some occasions to distinguish between Vikings engaged on trade and those who were intent on rape and pillage, although contemporary accounts (largely deriving from the Church) tend to equate the term 'Viking' with 'pirate', and hence shape our present-day view.

In the north, Scandinavian colonies spread from Shetland around the Western Isles of Scotland and to all coastal parts of Ireland. Indeed, by 830, Dublin and the surrounding area was to all intents and purposes a Viking state. The Orkneys and Faroe Islands were occupied at much the same time, and so too, by the end of the ninth century, Iceland. Vikings from Ireland sailed south to the Loire, to modern Portugal and southern Spain, and into the western Mediterranean. Swedish Vikings, meantime, had sailed across the Baltic and followed major river routes to Moscow and into the Arab world, and via Kiev to Constantinople. Whereas we tend to refer to peoples moving westwards from Scandinavia as Vikings, those travelling east became known as Varangians (hence the Varangian guard which was employed by the emperor at Constantinople), or as *Rhus* or *Rus* (our Russians), perhaps stemming from the Finnish word for the Swedes. All of these people travelled initially for purposes of trade, but it must soon have become apparent to many that in parts of western Europe, trade could be facilitated by the picking up of goods along undefended coasts. These included not only valuables such as furs and silver but also in some cases people, who could be traded in markets as slaves. All of these valuables – including books, and men and boys – were freely available in monasteries such as that at Lindisfarne.

Early sporadic raids and the westward spread of Vikings for settlement appear to have been wholly by men from Norway. From the 830s, however, Danes were also involved, and soon functioned in a more organised way than the small groups emanating from Norway. In 840 with the death of Louis the Pious, successor to Charlemagne, the Carolingian empire was split by civil war and the Danes took advantage of this dissention, forming themselves into large armies that moved into the mouths of rivers along the empire's northern coast. The pattern of attack now changed from short raids for plunder, limited to the summer months, with ships returning to Scandinavia for the winter, to more long-term attacks, with armies using local forced labour to build semi-permanent fortified camps for the winter months and forcing the payment of winter sustenance as tribute. Such camps were frequently on islands in river deltas, and these became the hall-mark of Viking strategy: camping on easily defended islands, with ships as a recourse in the event of a large land-based attack, and exacting tribute by posing a threat to the district. As far as England was concerned, the *Chronicle* reports raids of this kind on the Isle of Sheppey in the 850s and in Thanet in 865. The pattern was to be repeated in the later tenth-century Viking attacks, with which this book is principally concerned.

From the middle of the ninth century, the Danish army was engaged in campaigns throughout Europe, as far south as the Balearic Islands in the Mediterranean, across Provence and Tuscany in the late 850s and early 860s, before turning its attention to England. According to Abbo of Fleury's *Life of St Edmund*, composed in the tenth century supposedly from an eyewitness account, the Danish army which landed in England in 865/6 was led by men named as Ivar the Boneless and Hubba or Ubbi. They first attacked Northumbria and laid waste to it. Then half of the army led by Ivar sailed to East Anglia and overran that kingdom, eventually killing its king, Edmund (later canonised), in 869. Although we know from Norse sources that Ivar himself died at much the same time as Edmund, Danish leaders ruled Northumbria and East Anglia for the next half-century, and place-names show that Danish settlement throughout those areas was widespread even though the majority of the population was English. The *Anglo-Saxon Chronicle* also gives details of this invasion, but it has them landing in East Anglia and then riding into Northumbria the following year, returning to East Anglia in 869 and killing Edmund. Abbo's account is probably less reliable than the Chronicle entries, for his concern was primarily with the death of Edmund rather than the wider historical event, whereas the *Chronicle*, which itself was composed circa 890, is generally reliable for events in the second half of the ninth century. The latter also reports that rather than sailing to East Anglia, the army passed through Mercia, establishing winter quarters at Thetford in the very heart of East Anglia. Attacks on Mercia added to existing political problems in that kingdom which worsened as the century wore on. In 874 Burgred, the last legitimate Anglo-Saxon king of Mercia, was finally forced to flee and spent his remaining years in Rome. The Vikings established a puppet, Ceolwulf, to rule Mercia on their behalf, and with half of England now under Scandinavian domination, they turned their might on Wessex.

According to the *Chronicle*, Wessex had already felt the Viking threat, in the 830s, 840s and 850s. In 868, with the Vikings established in Nottingham, Burgred had asked for

West-Saxon help, but although it was given, he was forced to buy the Danes off. In 871 the Danish army had ridden to Reading and after a bloody encounter defeated the West Saxons led by their king, Æthelred, and his younger brother Alfred. Four days later, a second encounter between the same two armies led to an English victory. But just two weeks after that, the two forces met again at Ashdown in Berkshire where the Danes were successful again, although many were slain, including, according to the *Chronicle*, a number of named Viking leaders. Two weeks later the forces met at Basing in Hampshire, and many other similar large encounters followed. Clearly the Viking forces were highly mobile, and it would appear that they were able to outrun any significant army that the English could muster. Effectively they now had the freedom of Wessex, and the *Chronicle* suggests that all that the English leaders under Alfred could do was to harry them, while the king moved his army into positions where he could force them into battle. Most of these encounters occupied the length of the day before either reaching a stalemate or with the English obliged to retreat. This situation changed, however, in April when the king died and Alfred succeeded him. His accession was to prove the turning point in the fortunes of the English state as a whole.

King Alfred the Great, as he became known – the soubriquet deriving immediately from that of Charlemagne and more distantly from Alexander's – ruled Wessex and Kent from 871 to 899. In medieval terms this was a long reign, although Alfred's biographer, Bishop Asser, tells us that the king suffered from severe illnesses all his life, including piles which, although not life-threatening, was hardly something that a medieval king who spent much of his time on horseback would have relished. The length of his reign was not due, however, to the fact that Alfred was exceptionally long lived but that he came to the throne at a young age, being probably no more than twenty-two when he succeeded his

brother. The *Chronicle* entries for the last three decades of
the ninth century are a catalogue of Alfred's military and
naval successes, though these successes did not come easily at
first. Though not overtly stated, it is implied in the *Chronicle*
that for the first few years of his reign Alfred was assisted by
two circumstances. On the one hand, the Danish army went
north to Northumbria, and to the countries to the north
and west of it, i.e. Strathclyde and the kingdom of the Picts.
At the same time, Alfred seems to have bought a temporary
peace for Wessex by paying tribute to the invaders. This is
suggested, for instance, by the comment in annal 876 that
Alfred made peace with the Vikings in return for oaths
sworn on a sacred ring, but since the Vikings were then still
heathen at this time, such oaths would mean little without
a price having been paid for them to leave Wessex.

Although he had some minor successes in the very early
years of his reign, such as in the naval battle of 875 when he
defeated seven Viking ships, capturing one and forcing the
others to flee, it was not until 878 that Alfred's first major
victory occurred. After having suffered a number of setbacks
at the beginning of the year, forcing him, as the chronicler
puts it, to creep about with few followers in woodland
and marshes, he called to him all the men of Somerset,
Wiltshire and Hampshire, the heartland of his kingdom, and
joined battle with the Vikings at Edington in Wiltshire. The
Vikings were comprehensively defeated, and subsequently
were forced to sue for peace. This was granted in return
for them leaving Wessex and, more importantly in the long
run, accepting Christianity. No doubt this was a nominal
acceptance at first, and it was certainly accompanied by
Alfred's loading their leader Guthrum, king of East Anglia,
with treasure as he stood as sponsor for him at baptism.
But it was an important symbolic act. According to the
Chronicle, Mercia had been divided during the previous year
between Ceolwulf ruling in the west and the Danish army
in the east. Alfred accepted this division in the settlement

of 878 with Ceolwulf continuing to rule 'English' Mercia west and south of the line of Watling Street (the road from London to Chester), while the Danes ruled north and east of it. Alfred himself remained king of Wessex and Kent only at that time. Ceolwulf, however, died in 879, and in 880 Alfred moved north of the Thames into the old kingdom of the East Saxons, Essex, and in particular into its capital, the now derelict Roman site of London. By 886 he had rebuilt London and fortified it. At some point between these two dates, the *de facto* ruler of western Mercia, an ealdorman called Æthelred, submitted to Alfred in London, and the contract between them was underscored by Æthelred accepting Alfred's daughter, Æthelflæd, the so-called Lady (in our terms Queen) of the Mercians, in marriage. Alfred's charters subsequently style him 'King of the Anglo-Saxons' rather than merely king of the West Saxons, and it is clear that effectively Alfred ruled both kingdoms from that point, with Æthelred as his local administrator, although the Thames remained a significant political boundary until at least 1035. These developments were not necessarily symptomatic of Alfred's political ambitions but of the exigencies of defending the English, and particularly the West Saxon kingdom, against the Danish threat. The victory in 878, in other words, was a turning point in the history of England. Ultimately the Viking incursion into Wessex and the defeat of the invaders at Alfred's hands led to the unification of England as we know it today. The formation of the kingdom of the Anglo-Saxons, or 'greater Wessex', under Alfred's successors began in short with the battle at Edington.

Alfred's fortification of London was part of a series of similar defences built at the king's instigation to secure the kingdom from further attack. In 874, shortly after his accession and while Wessex was still under threat of falling under Scandinavian domination, like all the other Anglo-Saxon kingdoms, a large group of Vikings wintered in Mercia at a major Anglo-Saxon royal church at Repton on a bluff overlooking the river Trent, having rowed their ships up the river a hundred miles from the sea. By using dykes to link either end of the church to the river, they had built an extensive, impregnable position inland, very different from the island defences on which they usually depended. Alfred was an adaptable military commander, willing to draw ideas from any source including the tactics of his enemies, and he was quick to grasp the potential of this species of fortification. Although he may have learnt of the efficacy of fortresses from either Roman or Carolingian sources, it seems more than probable that he used such precedents near at home. In the course of his reign, he chose a series of natural or man-made sites to provide a ring of fortifications around his kingdom, some old Roman walled towns which control-led the Roman roads (Winchester and Chichester, besides London itself), where existing ruined walls could be rebuilt with the dressed Roman stone, some like Wallingford at other strategic sites. A number of these forts have now disap-peared, but most became the foundation of medieval towns where the original Anglo-Saxon grid-plan street pattern can still be seen. The primary purpose of these forts was, of course, defensive, to provide security for the surrounding rural population in the event of external or internal attack, but their ultimate importance was to provide a basis for urban living. Merchants began to assemble within the new walls, and markets grew up, which in turn offered kings an opportunity for regular taxation. The Old English word for such forts is *burh*, later spelt *buruh*, which gives 'borough' in present-day English, the history of the word paralleling the history of the settlement, i.e. a defensive site becoming an urban space. The forts were maintained by a system of taxation whereby the labour of the building and the costs of garrisoning were linked to the granting of land. For each hide of land, a hide being a family holding varying in acre-age, one man's service might be required, though in practice the requirement was probably less. Inevitably the nature and structure of these forts varied with the terrain. Old Roman sites had their walls repaired and may have been strengthened with wooden palisades, while natural hill-sites or other geological features may have had wooden defences alone. At significant river crossings such as Wallingford on the Thames, however, where there was neither natural defence nor pre-existing fortifications, the work had to be built from scratch. In addition to developing his physical defences, Alfred created a standing army, not an easy thing to accomplish in an essentially agrarian society. The *Chronicle* reports that in 893 Alfred divided his army into two, except for those engaged in garrisoning the forts, and he thus ensured that half his men were always on active service while the rest were at home cultivating the land. His final military achievement was the strengthening of the navy when, in 896, he ordered the building of a new design of ship, twice as long as the Viking boats to include more fighting men, but shallow-keeled for speed and manoeuvrability within the confines of the river estuaries that they were designed to defend. It was from this project that the tradition of the king as founder of the English navy derives, and it is interesting to note that the song 'Rule Britannia', with its refrain 'Britain rules the waves', comes from an eighteenth-century masque on the life of Alfred.

Alfred died in 899 and was succeeded by his son Edward the Elder (ruled 899-924) but the succession was disputed by his cousin Æthelwold, son of Alfred's brother and predecessor as king, Æthelred I. Having failed in a rebellion in Wessex itself, Æthelwold was accepted as their king by the Northumbrians and led them into breaking their peace with both Wessex and Mercia. In 904 he persuaded the East Anglians to invade Mercia and then Wessex, but this revolt was put down when Edward crossed into Cambridgeshire and brought them to a battle in 905 at which Æthelwold was killed. In the following years, the *Chronicle* reports that, in response to renewed threats from Northumbria and East Anglia, a combined force of West Saxons and Mercians fought with the Danish army in 909 and again in 910. When Ealdorman Æthelred of Mercia died in 911, western Mercia was ruled by Æthelflæd, Edward's sister, the first woman to exercise such power in Anglo-Saxon England, though the ultimate authority rested with the West Saxon crown. Æthelflæd was a very competent military commander in her own right, a true daughter of Alfred. First she strengthened her western defences with a series of forts along the Welsh border, having already rebuilt Chester with Æthelred in 907. With her western border secure, Æthelflæd moved against the Danes on her eastern flank, building fortresses at Tamworth, Stafford, Warwick, and other sites, and by 918 she had taken the Danish towns of Derby and Leicester, and obliged the men of York to enter into a truce.

At the same time her brother Edward was busy in the east. On the death of Ealdorman Æthelred, he had taken possession of London and Oxford 'and all the lands that belonged to them'. He then moved with his army north of London, building a fort at Hertford in 911 and strengthening it in 912, and later that year turning east into Essex and fortifying Witham near Maldon in 912. He fortified Buckingham in 914 and Bedford in 915. This gave the two English rulers a string of forts through an area previously controlled by Danes. In 916 Edward was back in Essex, fortifying Maldon, the highest point in the area, and in 917 was in Colchester, an old Roman site. The men of East Anglia then submitted to him without a fight. He then swung westwards into the northern fenlands and fortified Huntingdon during the same year and Stamford a year later in 918. In that year, however, Æthelflæd died, and Edward quickly had himself crowned king of Mercia in Tamworth, the capital of that kingdom, even though Æthelflæd had a daughter, Ælfwynn, whom evidence from charters suggests may have been being groomed by her parents as their successor.

The following year he moved to his new northern boundary, building forts at Thelwall on the Mersey estuary and Manchester in 919, and Bakewell in Derbyshire in 920. These new defences were necessary because of the growing power of Dublin as a Viking base and the need to cut the axis between Dublin and Viking York which relied heavily on the Mersey as a means of communication. Even so, settlements by Vikings from Dublin across Cheshire and in south Lancashire grew considerably during this period, as place-name evidence makes clear. But it cannot be doubted that Edward's success, coupled with that of his sister, was far-reaching: by the time of his death in 924 the midlands were ringed, as Wessex had been under his father, with fortified towns to the north, east and west (see Map 60), and the Viking settlers of the ninth century in the east midlands and in East Anglia had been integrated into a 'greater' Wessex.

What happened to the Viking settlers in England needs to be compared with the achievements of their counterparts in the western Carolingian empire, modern France. Large numbers of Vikings settled the area around Rouen in the last two decades of the ninth century, a region which became known as Normandy 'the land of the Norsemen', and by the end of the first decade of the following century France's King Charles the Simple was forced to grant them a duchy headed by Duke Rollo, the founder of the Norman dynasty. By the middle of the tenth century, the Norman dukes had extended their power to cover the area of the modern province. Like the settlers in England, they quickly accepted Christianity and spoke a northern variety of the local vernacular, French, although in England, since English and Norse were ultimately varieties of a single Germanic language and more or less mutually intelligible, Norse probably continued to be spoken for longer and influenced northern English dialects as it does to the present day. Political integration was far slower in France, however. Only in the early thirteenth century was Normandy absorbed into France and the separate duchy finally abolished, whereas in England the Vikings – at least as far north as the boundary of Northumbria – were under West Saxon control almost before Normandy came into being.

The story of West Saxon expansion continued in the next generation. Alfred's grandson Æthelstan (ruled 924–939) extended English rule beyond the line established by Edward which had included all the lands south of the Mersey and the Humber. Æthelstan, who had grown up in Mercia, succeeded to that kingdom on the death of his father in 924, but his half-brother Ælfweard inherited Wessex, effectively dividing Edward's kingdom again. Ælfweard survived Edward by only a matter of weeks, however, and the West Saxons accepted Æthelstan as their king in course of time, though the two kingdoms retained some form of independence for a number of generations. Edward had had many children, and Æthelstan married four of his half-sisters into major continental royal families, as a means of strengthening his position in Europe. Like both Æthelflæd of Mercia and his father Edward before him, he also made a treaty with the leaders of York (the effective rulers of Northumbria), but this broke down in 926 and the following year he took a southern-English army into Northumbria for the first time and received the submission of both the Northumbrians and the Scots from further north. Although he appears to have retained control of Northumbria for the rest of his reign, the Scots later rebelled, and he was forced to invade their lands in 934. Three years later, a major incursion into England by an army jointly led by Constantine king of Scots, Eugenius king of the northern Celtic kingdom of Strathclyde (modern Cumbria and points north as far as the Clyde), and Olaf, the Irish Viking king, with a combined force of Norsemen from Dublin and York, met Æthelstan and his half-brother and heir Edmund with forces from Mercia and Wessex at a battle at *Brunanburh*, an encounter celebrated in the *Chronicle* in an elaborate poem in heroic style. We cannot be sure where *Brunanburh* is – a number of possibilities have been suggested and the place-name is not infrequent in Anglo-Saxon England – but the most likely site is modern Bromborough on the southern bank of the Mersey on the Wirral peninsular. This location fits the poet's description of the escape of the vanquished Constantine across the Irish Sea to Dublin, and is both an appropriate place for an invasion of the heartland of the new polity of England (especially given its population of recently-settled Vikings from Dublin), and a typical position for an experienced Anglo-Saxon commander to choose for a battle since it is an easily defensible hill. We are told that Constantine escaped with few ships, although his son died on the battlefield, and Olaf too was killed. Æthelstan won a resounding victory and effectively became undisputed overlord of Britain. Despite minor disruptions in subsequent decades, the kingdom of England with its present boundaries was fixed in Æthelstan's day, and from that point it became an increasingly affluent European power.

For half a century after Æthelstan's victory at *Brunanburh*, England was safe from external attack. Though two years after the battle, there was a short period of instability when the inexperienced new king, Edmund, failed after Æthelstan's death to exercise his authority in the northeast midlands, and Viking leaders there led a rebellion, by the end of Edmund's brief six-year reign, his power was as great as that of his half-brother. He died unwontedly young, however, in 946, when he intervened in a quarrel at his court and was unintentionally stabbed. Neither of his two young sons was old enough to rule, and the crown consequently passed to his brother Eadred. The new king was sick, however, for the majority of his reign and rarely appeared at court, a situation which led to the management of the realm passing into the hands of the higher aristocracy, the regional earls known as ealdormen. A system of regional government had been established at an earlier date by King Alfred. In line with his father's practice in relation to his eldest brother, Alfred had given control of Kent to his son and successor Edward long before his death, while English Mercia was ruled by Ealdorman Æthelred and then by Æthelflæd. Prior to Ealdorman Æthelred's appointment, Alfred had used the term ealdorman to denote the most high-ranking royal official in a shire, and the extension of the title to the ruler of the whole of English Mercia was a clear indication of Æthelred's subordination to the king. As West Saxon control of an ever wider polity grew, so did the need for more ealdormen ruling an area greater than a shire, and in Eadred's reign we find powerful men in charge of Mercia and East Anglia, while Wessex itself was split between an ealdorman responsible for the west and another for the east. By and large, the most powerful ealdormen governed the older and larger kingdoms (Mercia, East Anglia and Northumbria), although some held earlier smaller kingdoms (such as Essex and Kent) consisting of no more than a single shire. But governance by the ealdormen did not mean that England was badly ruled. There appears to have been complete continuity in the objectives of the house of Alfred, for, indeed, most of the ealdormen were members of cadet branches of that house themselves. The policy of previous reigns was continued from one ruler to the next, and with the final expulsion in 954 by Eadred of the imaginatively named Erik Bloodaxe, the last Viking leader of York, not only did Northumbria become permanently part of England but no area of the kingdom was governed by a Viking until the Danish political conquest of the eleventh century.

Eadred died without issue in 955, and the crown reverted to Edmund's sons, by then old enough to take the throne. By the time that his second son Edgar became king of all England in 959, the peace was so widespread that he became known to the chroniclers as Edgar the Peaceable. However, early in the reign of Edgar's second son Æthelred (reigned 978 to 1016), Viking attacks began again. In one way this second wave of attacks mirrored the first, beginning with raids for plunder and developing into a process of political conquest and settlement. But the later attacks involved a smaller element of settlement and a much greater one of political control. England in the later tenth century had become one of the richest countries of Europe, and the relatively minor attacks of the 980s quickly turned into a major invasion led by political leaders intent on extending their power. The period of Viking settlement in England was over.

2

The Boats

By the nature of its geography, Scandinavia made sailors of its peoples. The inhabitants of present-day Norway in particular needed to fish, because they had so little land on which to farm; isolated communities kept in touch with one another by sea and even fought one another across the water; and boat-building consequently evolved throughout Scandinavia over many centuries. Sea-borne trade naturally followed on the construction of boats, and Scandinavian peoples became the principal traders of northern Europe in early medieval times, the Swedes eastwards because that was the way they faced, and the Norwegians and Danes westwards. The term 'viking', a Norse word of obscure origin, probably means inhabitant of a fjord or creek, but it came in time to mean 'sailor', although the Old English equivalent *wicing* always carried overtones of 'pirate'. Although it was land-based armies which afflicted England in the ninth and early eleventh centuries, it is principally sea-borne raiding with which Vikings are generally associated, and this chapter is concerned to establish all that is currently known about their boats.

We have been well served by archaeological remains for the reconstruction of Viking boats of the tenth and eleventh centuries. Buried and sunk ships have been recovered in such a complete state that everything about them can be seen except for the ropes and the sails, items that were naturally removed before a ship-burial or deliberate sinking. We also have a great many literary sources pertaining to Viking boats, including the sagas of the Norsemen themselves, which were not recorded until the thirteenth century although the tradition extends much further back in oral form, and other texts in English and Latin contemporary with the Viking raids. In Old Norse, the ships were generically referred to as *langskip*, literally translated as 'longships', which is the name by which they are now universally known even though different names were used in Norse to specify ships of different size and different uses. In English, the word *langscip* is used only once in the surviving records, in the *Anglo-Saxon Chronicle* entry for 897 where it is used of boats designed by King Alfred in response to the Viking ships which are there called *ascas*, 'boats made of ash-wood', a description which, as will be shown below, is probably technically inaccurate. Finally there are many surviving pictorial representations of longships, carved on wood or stone, including the ships represented on the Bayeux Tapestry which, although nei-

ther longships nor Viking in origin, are certainly very like
the Scandinavian longships in design and construction. Art
history then gives confirmation that the relatively few full
archaeological remains represent the norm of Viking ships
rather than the exception. It is the archaeological discoveries themselves, however, that give us our fullest and most
rounded picture of the boats, and of these three are particularly important: the magnificent Oseberg ship found in
1904 in a royal burial mound beside Oslo Fjord; the larger
but less elaborate and rather later Gokstad ship also in a
ship burial found on Oslo Fjord a quarter of a century
before Oseberg; and the five Skuldelev ships only relatively
recently discovered sunk in Roskilde Fjord in Denmark. In
date these seven vessels range from 800 to the mid-eleventh
century, but the construction of the boats hardly changes
in that time, and it is fair to assume that they represent a
cross-section of the vessels used by Vikings throughout the
period.

The Oseberg boat is undoubtedly the most splendid ship
to have survived from the Viking period. Dendroanalysis
tests on the timbers suggest that its burial took place in or
around 834 but that it was constructed a generation or two
before that, perhaps around the beginning of the ninth century. It thus dates from the very start of the Viking period.
It was clearly not built as an ocean-going vessel in that it is
far too shallow to be taken safely into the open sea, and it
is not therefore representative of ships that were involved
in early Viking raids on the English coast. It does have a
number of features, however, that give a useful indication
of the nature of Viking boat building. Made of oak, the
staple of northern shipbuilding up to Trafalgar, with beech
trimmings and a pine decking and mast, it was sumptuously
fitted out, possibly for royal progresses rather than practical
sailing purposes. Unusually in ship-burials and other graves
of this age, textiles and leather survived with it. The height
of the mast is uncertain but it is usually estimated at around

12 metres (40 feet), which would allow for a considerable
quantity of sail, perhaps as much as 70 square metres (84
square yards). We know very precisely, however, that it was
propelled by fifteen pairs of oars when it was not under sail,
and that the shallow keel and broad hull would make it an
easy ship to manoeuvre in the shallows when docking, an
important consideration in ensuring the impressive arrival
of a monarch displaying his power. Undoubtedly this was
a ship which was intended to make a statement. Its most
notable features were the highly decorated prow and stern,
each an extension of the keel but raised 5 metres (16 feet)
above the waterline. Both the front of the prow and the
back of the stern were jointed to the keel and highly decorated in a stylised interlace pattern. The same decoration
was employed on the inner edge of prow and stern, both
terminating in a wide outward spiral. However it may have
been used when it was operational, the ship has come down
to us as the most elaborate and expensive of grave-goods,
often assumed, by its precise – perhaps over-precise – dating,
to have been used for the burial of a queen.

The Gokstad ship was a larger and more formidable vessel, which dendrochronological tests suggest was
constructed around 890. This ship is therefore exactly contemporary with King Alfred, and its design suggests that it
was intended for pirating expeditions such as the *Anglo-
Saxon Chronicle* reports as taking place against England
during the ninth century. At over 23 metres (76 feet) long
and 5 metres (16 feet) wide, it is a little longer and slightly
wider than Oseberg, but with a much deeper keel and the
gunwale much further from the water-line, making it suit-
able for use in the open sea, even when fully laden (see
Plates 1 and 2). Unlike Oseberg, it is undecorated, giving
the clear impression that this is a working vessel. Again it is
largely built of oak with pine decking, and with thirty-two
oars against Oseberg's thirty. The fittings locating the foot of
the mast are extremely robust, braced by a four-ton block

of oak, suggesting its capability to withstand strong winds in open sea when under full sail. Such design features indicate a vessel capable of long voyages, and a replica has been sailed without difficulty across the Atlantic. The depth of its keel, however, suggests that it could not easily have been used in the shallower waters of estuaries or deep inland along the rivers that Vikings were known from literary sources to have used in England for some of their attacks. If not intended for inland raiding expeditions, then, for what was it designed? The obvious explanation would appear to be that it was intended for trade, but the archaeological remains include sixty-four shields ranged along the rack on the gunwale on each side of the vessel, equating precisely with the number of oars. In the ship-burial at least, this was a ship manned for war, and the assumption has to be that the oarsmen doubled as warriors. The fact that the decking is not fastened down as in Oseberg but is loosely fitted indicates a construction that allowed for a large storage area beneath the deck, suggesting that the ship's company expected to return from their voyages with a considerable supply of goods, whether acquired legally or not. Trade routes with large parts of Europe had become well established by the end of the ninth century, including regular sailings to Iceland.

In the same ship burial there were also found the remains of three smaller boats, ranging in size from 6.5 metres (21 feet) to just under 10 metres (32 feet). (The smallest boat might perhaps be compared with the dinghy being drawn behind Earl Harold's ship depicted on the Bayeux Tapestry in the scene representing his crossing to Normandy.) Since the skeleton found in the largest ship was that of a sixty-year-old man, it might be supposed that here we have the remnants of a fleet, with a commander's vessel and three subsidiary ones, the latter used perhaps for raiding inland with the main vessel reserved for heavy cargo on the voyage home. It is thus possible that the burial was that of a major captain who led raiding parties or trading expeditions, or

perhaps was engaged in both, through which he built up
the considerable wealth necessary for such an elaborate
funeral.

Gokstad should be seen in relation to a slightly later
ship of the early tenth century, found in 1935 in a burial
mound on the island of Funen in Denmark and known as
the Ladby ship. No timbers from the vessel have survived,
but a clear imprint of the ship in the soil reveals that it was
21.5 metres (70.5 feet) in length and nearly 3 metres (10
feet) wide, and thus, compared with Gokstad, a long thin
ship capable of considerable speed. It had seventeen pairs
of oars, slightly more than Oseberg or Gokstad. When first
discovered, it was disputed whether it was intended to bear
sail, or indeed whether it was capable of doing so, but a
Danish reconstruction which was sailed successfully across
the North Sea quickly settled that issue. There can be no
doubt that this was the type of warship that Alfred had
to contend with. Together with Gokstad, Ladby shows the
type of ship that was constantly harassing English shores
throughout the ninth century. The Oseberg and Gokstad
ships are superbly displayed in the University Museum of
Cultural Heritage at the University of Oslo, and offer an
excellent means of envisaging the great ships of the earlier
period of Viking expansion. Although they belong to the
first Viking age, their relevance to the later tenth century
lies in the information deducible from their excellent state
of preservation.

In a five-year archaeological investigation in Denmark
which began in 1957, another five ships were recovered
from the channel in which they had been deliberately sunk
in Roskilde Fjord, on the north side of Zealand, the island
on which Copenhagen now stands. From early in the eleventh century Roskilde was an important town, and the
sinking of the ships was no doubt part of an attempt in the
later eleventh century to defend the town from invasion by
an enemy fleet, either from Norway or a Baltic state (e.g.

the Wends who lived east of the Elbe), or even from a group engaged in a civil war within Denmark itself. The ships recovered were from a bank known as Skuldelev, and were named in order of their recovery from the site as Skuldelev 1, 2, 3, 5 and 6. Skuldelev 4 was a misnomer in that timber initially thought to belong to different vessel was later discovered to be part of Skuldelev 2, but the reassessment of the material took place only after 5 and 6 had been named. All of these ships belong to the later Viking period and are consequently of particular interest to the present survey. However, although they are all Viking-age ships, giving us the clearest possible indication of boat-building from the relevant period, they are very different from one another in size, design and purpose. It is consequently necessary to consider each of them in turn.

About seventy per cent of the hull of Skuldelev 1 has been preserved and it is possible to see its design and to make deductions not only about its place of origin but also about its use. There are marked differences between this ship and the boats described above. For instance, although much of the frame is of oak, particularly the keel, the sides – known as planking – are primarily of pine, though limewood was also used in its construction. The Skuldelev investigations as a whole have enabled a detailed examination of the timber used in the construction of all of the boats recovered, even allowing archaeologists to determine where the trees used were felled. Those deployed in the construction of Skuldelev 1 grew in south-west Norway, and since transport of the timber over any distance is unlikely, the ship was certainly built there. It had also been repaired, more than once, with oak from both Norway and Denmark, which means that it was in active use in both of those countries before it was used to block Roskilde Fjord. Dendroanalysis shows that it was built no earlier than 1025. The ship is relatively small, only 16 metres (52 feet) long, but with a width of almost 5 metres (16 feet), which is almost the same as the longer

Oseberg and Gokstad ships. It is apparent that this was a sturdy ship, intended for carrying heavy weights at slow speeds. Its repairs suggest that it spent most of its life in Scandinavia, although there is no reason why it should not have ventured into the open sea. Although there is provision for a few pairs of oars, the main means of propulsion was clearly the sail, and the vessel was patently not manoeuvrable enough for warfare, even though there is an arrow-hole in the bow. Perhaps cargo ships were used in some circumstances as adjunct vessels in war or raiding, either for conveying troops or more probably for carrying booty derived from raids.

Contemporary with Skuldelev 1 is Skuldelev 6, a small 10 metre (33 foot) boat built in the same area of Norway again with an oak frame and pine planking. It is even better preserved than Skuldelev 1, so much so that it has been established that it was initially built as a fishing vessel with up to twelve oars, but that at some point it was converted as it got older into a small cargo boat by an adaptation to its gunwale allowing it to carry greater weight without being in danger of taking water in over the sides. Skuldelev 3 and 5 are built in contrast to both the two previous boats from Danish timber, but very different from each other in character. Skuldelev 3 is midway in size between 1 and 6, about 14 metres (46 feet) long, and like them was a cargo ship. Built around 1040 of fine quality Danish oak, almost all of which survives, its carrying capacity was a good deal less than that of Skuldelev 1, although more than that of the converted Skuldelev 6. These three Skuldelev ships show the range of vessels available in eleventh-century Denmark. It is Skuldelev 5 and 2, however, that are the most exciting among these discoveries. Like the other Skuldelev ships, Skuldelev 5 belongs to the eleventh century, but at over 17 metres (56 feet) in length and only 2.5 metres (8 feet) in width, and with a capacity for thirteen pairs of oars, it is a fast warship of the type that plagued the English in the ninth

century and again in the late tenth. Of all the ships in the
Skuldelev site, this is the most valuable for the purposes of
this discussion (Plates 3–5).

Timber analysis proves that Skuldelev 5 was built in
Denmark around 1030. Although the bottom of its hull
was constructed of fresh oak, the planking on its sides is
of reused pine and ash from earlier ships. Even the new
oak is of a poorer quality than that used for Skuldelev 3.
In Skuldelev 5 older oar-holes have been covered over and
new ones drilled. This is a workmanlike ship in which the
reuse of timber shows that it was intended for practical
rather than show purposes, although the standard of crafts-
manship in the construction, as with that of all the boats
recovered, is high. Repairs suggest that it had a long life even
in its final form, and that it probably remained in use for
the three or four decades up to the time of its sinking. Not
only does it give us an insight into the design and size of
ship that formed the core, in all probability, of viking raids
on England but also it shows that the demand for such boats
in the early eleventh century was so great that boat-builders
were forced to cannibalise older boats for their materials. It is possible, indeed, that the ship was built to satisfy
the legal demands in the tenth and eleventh centuries that
each region should supply the king at need with a manned
warship, with the cost of building as well as of supplying and manning the vessel falling on the local population
(see Chapter 3). It is interesting that alone of the Skuldelev
boats, Skuldelev 5 has a single plank of ashwood among its
repairs. In the English records and some continental Latin
ones Viking ships are referred to as 'ash-ships'. Since the
ash plank here is part of the reused wood, it is possible
that such terminology has a basis in historical fact and that
ninth-century ships were indeed made of ash. Because the
boat was old when it was scuttled and because much of its
timber was probably already decayed, the remains are much
less substantial than those of the cargo boats, but almost all

the timber from the port side is preserved, and fortunately for the state of our knowledge, this includes both the oar-holes and the shield-rack.

The final wreck in the Skuldelev barrier is Skuldelev 2, the jewel in the crown of all the Skuldelev ships, although sadly only about one fifth of it is preserved. It is the jewel in the sense that it is the remnant of a magnificent warship, around 30 metres (almost 100 feet) in length but less than 4 metres (13 feet) in width and with provision for thirty pairs of oarsmen. Its dimensions suggest that it would have been capable of very high speeds, extremely long but very narrow and with a draught of less than a metre (3 feet), and hence able to skim through the water like a larger version of a modern racing shell (Plate 6). It was built almost entirely of Irish oak, and therefore it must be assumed it was constructed in Dublin, around 1040. The rowing positions are slightly closer together than is the case with other warships, which might suggest either that the sail was principally relied upon for propulsion and that this is primarily an ocean-going vessel, or that there was a need for speed in close quarters or perhaps a desire for as many oarsmen – who doubled as warriors – as possible. Skuldelev 2 was repaired, again with Irish oak, twenty years after its construction, which testifies to continued use in Ireland over a long period before it made its journey to Denmark where it was scuttled around 1070. Although its late date makes it unlikely that this is a ship which was used against Anglo-Saxon England in the second wave of Viking attacks of the later tenth and early eleventh centuries, it was perhaps used in the reign of Edward the Confessor or in the early Norman period when Irish Norse activity continued to be high. King Harold II's sons, for example, are known to have fled to Ireland after their father's death at the battle of Hastings.

Other archaeological investigations of recent times have added yet more to our knowledge. At Hedeby, a major trading port on the southern border of Denmark, remains of Viking-age ships were discovered in the harbour in 1953, although the timbers were not investigated until 1979. One of the ships, Hedeby 1, was a warship similar in design and dimensions to Skuldelev 2; in other words it was about 30 metres (100 feet) long and under 3 metres wide (10 feet), and carried thirty pairs of oars. Its remains are incomplete because it was used as a fire ship around the year 1000, intentionally set alight to protect the town during a sea-borne attack. Nonetheless, enough survives for it to be deduced that it was of carefully timbered Danish oak, even better chosen and prepared than that used in Skuldelev 2, a fact which, together with its size, suggests that it was commissioned by a very wealthy man, perhaps even a king. It was built around 985 and therefore could well have been used in an invasion of England at the end of the tenth century. The most recent discovery is even more remarkable. In 1997, in the course of dredging Roskilde harbour in the building of the magnificent ship museum which now houses the Skuldelev remains, a number of Viking-age boats were found in the mud. A group of three cargo boats similar in dimension to Skuldelev 1 included one dating from the mid-eleventh century (Roskilde 3), and with them was yet another boat, now named Roskilde 6, which proved to be the most exciting discovery of all, the largest long-boat yet found, fully 35 metres (115 feet) in length, with provision for thirty-four pairs of oars. Again built of oak, this ship has been dated to *circa* 1025, the time when Cnut (Canute) ruled England, Denmark and, for a time, both Norway and southern Sweden. For a comparison of the relative sizes of these longships, see Figure 71. Before the discovery of these vessels, historians were highly sceptical of literary accounts of longships of sixty oars or more, such as Olaf Tryggvason's boat known as 'Long Serpent' which was reputed to have had thirty-four pairs. Though Olaf was active in England at the end of the tenth century, the written sources of his life are of Norse origin and date from the thirteenth. Historians have consequently assumed that reports of the size of his 'Long Serpent' were as legendary and as over-written as other aspects of his life. Recent archaeology, however, has transformed our understanding. With three Viking warships of 30 metres (100 feet) and upwards having already been discovered, it is obvious that, while they may not have been commonplace, such magnificent ships were in regular use in the North Sea in the late tenth and eleventh centuries, and thus they formed an integral part of the second Viking age in England. Linguistic evidence, moreover, can be added to the archaeological record, the two lending each other weight. In Norse, the term *snekkja* refers to a small fast ship of the type of Skuldelev 5, and it is probably this that is referred to in the *Anglo-Saxon Chronicle* entry for 897 as *ascscip* 'ash-ship'. The term *snacc* is borrowed into English in the mid-eleventh century (but not earlier) for such a small vessel. The Norse term for the true longships of the Roskilde 6, Hedeby 1 and Skuldelev 2 type is *skeið*, and this appears in English records as *scegð* (with the same pronunciation 'skeith') in the *Chronicle* report that in 1008 King Æthelred ordered a warship with forty oars to be commissioned from every 300 hides of land. The fact that such a tax was levied is proved by a will made soon afterwards by Ælfwold, bishop of Crediton, who died in 1012 leaving a sixty-four-oared *scegð* to his lord. By 1008, it would appear, warships with forty to seventy oars were widespread.

As well as imaginatively displaying all the remains of the Skuldelev ships, the Viking Ship Museum at Roskilde has built exact replicas of all of them since 1984, giving a clear sense of what they looked like and how they performed at sea (Plates 7–9). The reconstructions are made available to visitors to allow them to take trips out into the fjord, thus giving them an intimate sense of the sea-worthiness of the vessels, as well as an opportunity to row and sail them. The reconstructed warships are capable of speeds up to an impressive fourteen knots. Anyone wishing to be a modern-day Viking can enjoy the experience of these boats, though without the pleasures of pillaging and looting. More importantly, perhaps, the museum offers a chance to see boat building in Viking fashion in action, using replicas of the tools available to the original boat-builders, tools which are very precisely shown on the Bayeux Tapestry as William prepares for his invasion of England.

The archaeological and literary evidence further reveals that in two and a half centuries from 800 to 1050, i.e. Oseberg to Skuldelev 2, the building of warships in Norse areas changed hardly at all. The rudder was on the starboard side towards but not at the back of the vessel, the etymology of starboard, Old English *steorbord*, being literally 'the plank for steering', referring to the rudder itself. The rudder was strapped to the frame of the ship with a leather belt strengthened with ropes, and protruded above the gunwale. The tiller was slotted into the upper end of the rudder which then could be swivelled within the leather band. The helmsman stood on the aft deck and faced forward. Both prow and stern were elongated, and ended in a scroll or animal device, as we see from drawings, either carved in wood or in ornamental metalwork. Some examples of the metal finial are thought to survive to modern times as weather vanes on church steeples. Each gunwale had a shield-rack on which the shields were hung overlapping each other. Oars were intended for a single rower and had narrow blades which modern experience suggests is best for open sea rowing. The oarsmen sat side by side in pairs, and texts refer to the ships by the number of rowing seats, a fifteener being manned by thirty men. The best ropes were made of sealskin, as we are told in an account in Old English by a Norwegian trader at the court of King Alfred, a man named Ohthere (Norse Ottar) who tells of his journey from northern Norway around the North Cape and into the White Sea. But archaeology suggests that ropes were also made of braided strips of willow bark. The single sail was square and made of dyed wool, with leather strapping, and in the larger ships it had a timber yard pulling it up square. Raising the sail would have taken considerable strength, but this might have been aided by a system of pulleys. Pictorial evidence suggests how it might have been furled. It could certainly be turned to different wind positions, and tacking was well within the scope of the vessel. The ships, in other words, were extremely well adapted either to sailing on the open sea or to estuary and river work. One particularly distinctive feature of the warship Skuldelev 5 is that traces of an inscribed acanthus-leaf pattern can be seen on one of the planks, a design widely known from stone carvings and other artwork found throughout the British Isles and Scandinavia in the late tenth and early eleventh centuries. The remains of this wreck are too slight for much detail to be seen, but the acanthus-leaf design is indicative that the sides of the warships were carved and probably painted. The Oseberg ship is, as has been described, very ornate, and there are carvings on the Gokstad tiller, but the decoration on Skuldelev 5 shows that all warships, even the most workaday ones, are likely to have been decorated. Together with the colourful sail, a warship under full rig must have been an impressive and – for a population who had felt the might of Viking aggression – a terrifying sight.

An account of a fleet of warships survives in an eleventh-century text known as the *Encomium Emmae Reginae*. Emma was the second wife of King Æthelred, a Norman princess whom he married in 1002. After his death in 1016 she married Cnut, the Dane who ruled England from 1016 to 1035. By Cnut she had a son, Harthacnut, who ruled from 1040 to 1042, and by Æthelred she had two sons, one of whom reigned as Edward the Confessor from 1042 to 1066. She was thus at the centre of English court life for more than half a century. She also had a few periods of exile, however: in 1014 together with Æthelred, when she was back in Normandy, and after Cnut's death in 1035 when she took refuge in Flanders. It was soon after her return from Flanders in 1040 that she commissioned a Flemish monk to write her history, in an account which concentrates particularly on the Danish conquest in 1013-1016. In this context, Book II of the *Encomium* describes Cnut's fleet as he prepared to invade England in 1015, a fleet reported as consisting of 200 ships. The encomiast's style is hyperbolic, but some sense of the elaborate decoration of the boats can be derived from his account:

> So great... was the ornamentation of the ships that the eyes of the beholders were dazzled, and to those looking from afar they seemed of flame rather than of wood. For if at any time the sun cast the splendour of its rays among them, the flashing of arms shone in one place, in another the flame of suspended shields. Gold shone on the prows, silver also flashed on the variously shaped ships. So great, in fact, was the magnificence of the fleet that if its lord had desired to conquer any people, the ships alone would have terrified the enemy, before the warriors whom they carried joined battle at all.

It is difficult to calculate with any certainty how many men were involved in Viking attacks at any period. Reports in the English sources of small numbers of ships can probably be relied upon, for example, in the *Chronicle* we are told that Alfred fought seven ships in 875, two in 882, sixteen in 885 (all captured and so presumably this is a reliable statistic), and six in 896. Since entries for all these years were made within the lifetime of the chroniclers, the first three by 891 in the copy that survives, the last very soon after the event, it is almost certain that they are accurate. Since much of the material in the early *Chronicle* is likely to have originated in Alfred's own court, this gives even greater credence to the figures. By contrast it is extremely unlikely that the high numbers reported elsewhere in the Chronicle can be trusted in the same way. By its nature, chronicle writing

needs to give a sense of authenticity, and part of this might
be achieved by recording precise information such as exact
figures, but there are signs that we are sometimes dealing with verisimilitude rather than reality. The chroniclers'
informants would hardly be in a position, for example, to
count exact numbers in the case of large fleets. In 993 it is
reported in one version of the *Chronicle* (which survives in
a number of related but differing forms) that ninety-three
ships attacked south-east England, but this number curi-
ously coincides with the annal number. In other surviving
versions, the fleet is reported to have attacked in 994 and
is said to have consisted of ninety-four ships, heightening
the coincidence with the annal number. The *Chronicle* has
similar examples of such coincidences in other contexts. For
example, as early as 784 it is reported that in a palace rebellion led by Cyneweard, brother of a former king, the reign-
ing king Cynewulf was killed together with eighty-four of
his men. Although precise numbers were very important
to the chroniclers then, too much reliance should not be
placed on them. What can safely be assumed, however, is that
there is a marked difference between an attack by a Viking
raiding party, where the number of ships is probably accurately recorded, and a significant fleet where the numbers
cited by the chronicler are intended to give a sense of a large
army but are not meant to be literally understood.

   In 896, just a few years before his death, King Alfred
ordered his shipwrights to create a new design of warship for defence against the Danes of East Anglia and
Northumbria who were attacking the southern coast of
Wessex with ships which, according to the *Chronicle*, 'they
had built many years previously'. Amongst other new features, these English ships were 'very nearly twice as long as
the others; some had sixty oars, some more'. This affords
contemporary confirmation of the archaeological record
(i.e. that the usual size of Danish warship was thirty oars),
but it also shows that Alfred believed that the satisfactory

defence of the realm required the use of much larger vessels of the size of Skuldelev 2. The *Chronicle* entry continues with an account of the limited success of this strategy in the only detailed record that we have of a sea battle between the two forces. Six Danish ships attacked the Isle of Wight and did great damage along the coast as far as Devon. King Alfred sent nine of his new ships against them and these caught up with the invaders in an estuary where the tide had ebbed. Three of the Danish ships came out to meet the English, but the other three had been beached and their sailors had disembarked and were engaged in pillaging inland. Of the three ships that engaged the English, two were taken and their occupants killed while the third escaped with just five survivors on board. The size of the ships in the defensive force paid off in this encounter, but told against the English perhaps in what followed. During the sea-battle, in the narrow confines of the estuary, three of the English longships became stranded on the side of the channel where the Danish ships were beached, but the rest ran aground on the opposite side and their occupants were unable to help their companions. When the Vikings returned from their raiding inland, neither side could re-launch their ships and a land battle took place. A great many of both English and Danes were killed (the *Chronicle* numbers sixty-two English and 120 Danes), but the incoming tide eventually reached the Danish ships, and they were able to row away while the longer English boats were still stranded. The Danes were so depleted in number, however, that they got no further than Sussex, where they were again beached by wind and tide, and the men were captured by the defending forces and hanged. If the numbers reported to have been killed in this fight were to be taken at face value, it would imply that there were more than forty men on board each of the three Danish ships whose occupants took part in the encounter on land. This would not accord with the specified number of oars in the *Chronicle* description of Alfred's new ships but

it does tally with the number of oars and shields in Gokstad.
It is possible that one at least of the Viking ships was larger
than thirty oars, but more likely that some of the raiding
party included men from the three ships which fought in
the engagement at sea while the rest were left to guard the
whole of the Danish fleet. However, the *Chronicle*, as we
have seen, is very unreliable in its account of large numbers. The given number of Danish dead is coincidentally
similar to twice the number of the English losses, giving
the impression of a great victory although at considerable
cost. But since the list of English dead is prefaced by the
names of five notable men (including two royal officials),
it is conceivable that the record of the English casualties is
accurate, and although it is not possible to give too much
credence to the precise number of Viking dead, it would
appear that they exceeded the English casualties. All in all,
it would seem that Alfred's plan to construct larger vessels
capable of carrying a greater number of men paid off in
the land encounter between two groups of three ships, for
though the English losses were significant, the defenders did
succeed in defeating the Vikings comprehensively.

The report of Alfred's decision to build sixty-oar boats
which were twice the length of the Danish ships indicates
the chronicler's view of the size of Danish vessels in the
ninth century, a view supported by archaeology with the
Ladby ship and Skuldelev 5. By the end of the tenth century,
however, England faced a new threat. Not only were sea-
borne attacks resumed but also the work-horses of renewed
Viking raids like Ladby and Skuldelev 5 were now accompanied by true longships, 'Long Serpent' boats like Hedeby
1, Roskilde 3 and Skuldelev 2. It is to these and the men
aboard them that the next chapter will turn.

3

The Return of the Vikings

In 975, on the eve of the death of King Edgar the Peaceable, great grandson of Alfred the Great, England within its present-day boundaries was internally and externally free from attack, prosperous, united under a strong monarch and an equally strong church. After his death, the country became politically divided with factions supporting one or other of his two young sons. Those on the side which supported the elder of the half-brothers, known to history as Edward the Martyr, were aligned with the Church and saw themselves as the true inheritors of Edgar's policy, while the others, who supported the younger brother Æthelred, sought to deprive the Church of the wealth it had acquired under Edgar. It is possible that these internal divisions were perceived as an opportunity by those overseas who saw an opening to prey on England's wealth, but it is much more likely that Vikings who roamed western Europe throughout this period but who had been kept at bay from English soil by the firm government of the country under Edgar now found that it was possible to gain access to the kingdom's riches. It was also apparent that much of England's wealth lay in a material form which could be easily transported, and hoards of such materials were widespread throughout the land. Late in Edgar's reign, a new national coinage had been established, and subsequently the designs on the basic monetary unit, the silver penny, were altered every six years (see Plates 11–14). The exchequer used each reissue of the coinage to gather taxation: old coins became invalid and had to be exchanged for new, and fewer coins of the new issue were given in return for the old (perhaps as high as fifteen per cent less), while a charge was made on the moneyers for the centrally distributed dies. For the system to be effective, there had to be an effective means of distributing the new coins, and this resulted in a supply chain whereby nowhere in the country was more than a short riding distance from a mint (see Map 62). Hundreds of millions of silver pennies were in circulation, which meant that moneyers needed a ready quantity of raw materials. Invaders could thus be sure that within a relatively short radius of the point at which they landed, wherever that might be, there was a sure supply of silver.

Just three years after his father's death, Edward, then probably no more than fifteen years of age, was murdered as he arrived at a manor on the site of what is now the ruined Corfe Castle in Dorset. His death was ordered, presumably, by a member of his brother's party, although how high up the political system the treason was sanctioned is not clear. The most significant result of this event for English political history is that his brother Æthelred became king at just twelve years of age, and power passed, as it had in the time of Eadred their great-uncle, into the hands of his nobles. On this occasion, however, the nobles were radically divided, and those who had supported Edward were relatively disenfranchised. Those who now wielded authority were concerned more with the redistribution of land than with the needs of the state, especially the rich acres which had been gained by the Church in Edgar's day. England was vulnerable to external aggression for the first time for many years.

Just how vulnerable it had become was demonstrated early in Æthelred's reign. Two years after his succession, after more than thirty years of peace, Viking raids began again. The *Anglo-Saxon Chronicle* reports that in 980 there were three Viking forays into England: Southampton was attacked by a fleet 'and the citizens mostly killed or taken captive'; Thanet in eastern Kent was ravaged, although not necessarily by the same men; and Cheshire was attacked by 'a fleet from the north', a phrasing which clearly implies a different group. Southampton was then a fortified town, and the major port on the south coast. In King Æthelstan's day it had had two mints, and minting was still in process at the end of the century. It has been estimated that the town had a population of between 3,500 and 5,000 in the year 800, and it must have grown considerably in the course of the intervening centuries. Large towns in late Anglo-Saxon England were thriving, bustling places where commerce and manufacturing industries were concentrated. They were occupied by considerable numbers of tradesmen and merchants, all with stocks of goods of value to Vikings. Manorial estates in the surrounding area each had a town house where produce from the lord's land could be sold, and his animals butchered to provide the townsfolk with fresh meat, and where the lord lived when occasion required. The townspeople and their places of trade were, at least in theory, well protected. Southampton had been fortified by King Alfred, and its sacking was thus a significant event. The Viking incursion suggests that its defences were either unmanned or poorly maintained, perhaps both, and its citizens paid the price of that neglect.

The attack on Southampton is described in the *Anglo-Saxon Chronicle*. The *Chronicle* survives in seven manuscript copies written by a series of scribes from the end of the ninth century until the mid-twelfth in different monastic centres. The copies have some material in common but all have differences which often relate to their area of transmission, and they are known by the letters A to G, which refer, in the case of the first five (which are the significant ones for the purposes of this study) to the date of their composition. Three versions report the attack on Southampton, of which only version C includes it under the entry for 980. D and E, by contrast, report it under the annal for 981 and add the information that just seven Viking ships were involved. It has been suggested that annals 978–982 in the C version were compiled at Abingdon where the C manuscript is usually agreed to have been written, but there are differences in style between these entries and those elsewhere in this chronicle, as well as marked differences of content between the C version and that in DE which suggest that C's annals did not derive from the common stock material of the CDE in other annals. C's use of the mid-tenth-century form of the name *Suðhamtun* for the town as against the older form *Hamtun* found in DE in itself shows independence, and the interest in southern affairs, and in particular in south-western prelates and places has been seen by some historians as proof that the material was compiled in the Wessex heartland, perhaps at Winchester. Given the centrality of Southampton to Wessex, the date of 980 should probably be accepted, and the fact that C makes no mention of the number of ships allows the possibility that more than seven were involved. Even if only seven took part, however, they might well have held up to 300 warriors, quite enough men to wreak havoc on an unarmed civilian population. Again, only the C version reports that most of the townspeople were killed or captured, but there is no reason to doubt the veracity of this. We know from other sources that this was the usual outcome of a Viking raid on a civilian population. Those who were captured might be ransomed if their families were sufficiently wealthy; otherwise they would be carried off to be sold in European slave markets.

Only C reports the attacks on Thanet and Cheshire, but again there is no reason to doubt the truth of the accounts. The northern fleet attacking Cheshire almost certainly stemmed from Norse settlements in Ireland, the Isle of Man or the Western Isles, areas from which Viking attacks on the Welsh coast originated throughout the 970s. Thanet, a large island off the north-east coast of Kent, now joined to the mainland, had been frequently subject to attacks by Vikings in the first wave of raiding. Since it has steep cliffs on the north and east coasts, but branches of the river Stour on its south and west side, the Vikings presumably sailed up the broad Stour estuary, but there was no major settlement in the area after the monastery of Minster-in-Thanet was destroyed by Danish attacks in the mid-ninth century. It seems unlikely therefore that the fleet which attacked Southampton and took rich pickings there would have gone on to invade the rural backwater of Thanet, however valuable the farmland of the area. The conclusion must be that 980 saw attacks in different parts of England by three different groups. Similar attacks continued in the following year, although again they are reported only by chronicle C. This chronicle's interest in the south-west is evident in the information that it supplies that St Peter's monastery in Padstow, Cornwall, was ravaged, and that the Vikings did great damage along the coasts of

Devon and Cornwall. Again in 982 it tells that 'three ships of vikings arrived in Dorset and ravaged Portland'. It may be that such attacks had become so endemic by the time that the eleventh-century chronicler of the DE version was writing that he did not think it worthwhile to report them, whereas they were a new phenomenon for the western chronicler of the 978–982 annals of C. In any event, when the independent entries of C ended in 982, such reports largely disappear from the record. Only one further attack is reported in the *Chronicle*, this time by CDE together, a large battle at Watchet on the coast of Somerset in which Goda the thegn of Devon and a large number of men were killed.

Like the earlier attacks on Cheshire and the coasts of Wales, it is probable that those on Padstow, which is on the northern coast of Cornwall, and on unspecified sites on the coasts of Devon and Cornwall in 981, together with the battle at Watchet on the Bristol Channel in 988 all involved Vikings based in the British Isles, whereas the attack on Dorset in 982, like others on the south coast in 980, were probably by Danes, either from Denmark itself or from bases in Normandy. That the Danes used such bases in Normandy is known from negotiations between England and Normandy which took place in 990. Sigeric, who became archbishop of Canterbury in 990, went to Rome that year for his pallium or badge of office, and while there, on behalf of Æthelred, appears to have persuaded the Pope (John XV) to intervene in a dispute between the two countries over harbouring Danes. A papal envoy visited first England and then Normandy later that same year, and an agreement was subsequently drawn up between the parties designed to prevent this situation recurring. Despite his reputation for bad governance, Æthelred's diplomatic mission of 990 seemed to have succeeded. The agreement did not affect attacks by Vikings either from Ireland or the Western Isles, however, nor could it stop incursions from Scandinavia. Given the geographical situation of the major attack which took place in 991, when a large force sacked Ipswich before moving on to Maldon, where it was confronted by an English army led by Byrhtnoth, ealdorman of Essex, it seems likely that this came directly from either Norway or Denmark or both.

The motives underlying the raids of the early 980s may not solely originate in political instability in England, however. Denmark too was in ferment at the time. During this period, King Harold Bluetooth imposed his rule on a country which in the first half of the tenth century was split between a number of ruling factions, each of which controlled a relatively small area. The runic tombstone erected by Harold for his father Gorm the Old at Jellinge on the Danish mainland of Jutland states:

> King Harold commanded this memorial to be made in memory of his father and mother, Gorm and Thyre, that same Harold who won all Denmark and Norway for himself, and converted the Danes to Christianity.

Harold himself had converted to Christianity around 965, the first Danish ruler to do so. Jellinge, where Gorm's tombstone was situated, is one a series of circular fortresses built by Harold throughout the country in 980/981, which were in effect military training establishments. He also built bridges and military-style roads which enabled him to control the entire populace. It has often been argued that the imposition of Christianity by Harold on the Danes was the principal motive for many of them taking to their boats and sailing westwards to look for treasure elsewhere. Certainly the central government that he instigated is likely to have been instrumental in this respect, but changes in the state religion seem a less likely explanation, although a combination of these factors might account for the westward expansion of the Danes to Iceland, Greenland and North America. More

ominously for England, he created an important legacy for
his son, a unified and centrally controlled kingdom with
potentially significant military resources.

Just as important as local political events in Denmark,
however, were larger economic causes. In the middle of the
tenth century, the supply of silver from the east began to dry
up. Princes in Kiev had begun to disrupt Scandinavian trade
routes between the Baltic and the Volga, and the ready influx
of money into northern lands began to decline. Although
it was principally the Swedes who were engaged in trade
with the east, the economy of Denmark was affected too,
and by 970 the situation had become serious. This may be
the major factor behind the search for silver from the west,
particularly from rich, undefended sites in England, and
it offers a further explanation for the sudden renewal of
small-scale attacks in the mid-980s. The political situation
in Denmark, moreover, took a new turn during the 980s
when Harold's son, Swein Forkbeard, rebelled against his
father and expelled him from the kingdom. Swein inherited
a unified realm, and one Harold believed to be so secure that
he was able to leave it to conquer Norway, as the runestone
to his father claims. Swein was more ambitious still. He took
his army to England during the 990s.

It seems that he was not the only one to do so. Four
versions of the *Chronicle* record events in the first half of
the 990s. Versions CDE agree in stating under the annal
for 991 that Ipswich was ravaged, and very soon afterwards
Ealdorman Byrhtnoth was killed at Maldon. These three
copies of the text were all made in the eleventh century or
later, and are dependent on a lost version, made presumably early in the same century. Version A, which was made
at Winchester, was copied around the year 1000, closer to
the events recorded, and has more information than the
others about this raid, noting that the fleet first attacked
Folkestone and then Sandwich in Kent before sailing round
to Ipswich. Unfortunately all of this information appears in

the annal for 993, whereas it is clear from the fact that there is no sign of Byrhtnoth in the historical record after 990 (he signs no legal documents after that date) that the battle was indeed fought in 991. This does not invalidate the extra information supplied by the A version that other towns were sacked before Ipswich. A careful examination of the A manuscript reveals that the information entered under annal 993 had been added after the original text had been set out, presumably as the material for the annal in question came to hand (see Plate 38 and the plan of the page in Figure 73). It may be assumed that the scribe simply wrote the entry against the wrong annal number, 993 for 991. The extra material may derive from a fuller source than that available to the CDE chronicler, because A has more information on other topics. A problem arises, however, in that some of this information overlaps with material that CDE has under the annal for 994, suggesting that there may be some conflation in A between events occurring in different years.

The overlapping material concerns a certain Anlaf, which is the Old English spelling of the Norse name Olaf, who is described by A as the leader of the invasion of 993 and who the CDE chronicle names as the head of an invasion in 994. It is clear that this refers to Olaf Tryggvason, a man whose life was so extraordinary that it was turned into legend, recorded in the saga *Ólafs saga Tryggvasonar* which survives in a number of versions in manuscripts of the thirteenth and fourteenth centuries, all of which seem to stem from an oral tradition of the late twelfth century. Similar accounts of his life also appear in some Latin histories of Norway and of the early Norwegian kings. Such late sources offer unreliable evidence of the actual life of this Viking but are testimony to the scale of the man and his deeds. Much closer to Olaf's own time, and consequently rather more reliable in terms of historical fact, are the words of Olaf's own court poet in his *Ólafsdrápa*, apparently composed in 996. From a combination of these sources together we can

determine something of Olaf's life, and may begin to dis-
entangle fact from myth. He was born in southern Norway,
son of Tryggve Olafsson, one of many so-called kings of the
region, who was probably no more than a local chieftain,
although a grandson of the first king of Norway (Harold
Fairhair, died 933). Olaf and his mother went into exile
in Sweden after the murder of his father, and Olaf later
travelled around the Baltic, reputedly spending some years
as a slave in Estonia before arriving at the court of Vladimir
the Great who ruled Kiev from 980 to 1015 and was the
first Christian ruler of Russia. From Russia Olaf went to
Poland and married a princess, Geira, and ruled half of
that country with her until she died in 990. The next year,
that of the battle of Maldon, Norse sources indicate that
he was leading raiding parties in northern territories of
the Carolingian empire and, subsequently, in England. The
records are unclear, however, about where precisely he was
in England during that year. Mention is made of his being
in 'the south' before he sailed on to Northumbria, and this
seems likely, given that he came to England from the continent, but it does not supply clear evidence that he was
present at Maldon. Though the A chronicle describes him
as head of ninety-three ships attacking the coast in 993, this
looks suspiciously like the account of him leading ninety-
four ships in the CDE chronicle annal for 994. There is no
doubt that he was raiding in southern England by 994 and
that King Æthelred negotiated a treaty with him in that year
by which he became Christian and left the country, never to
return (an event widely recorded), but that does not solve
the question of whether he was in the south-east in 991.

There are many more significant questions to be answered
in relation to the Viking force that arrived at Maldon and
the nature of its organisation. Most importantly, why did the
Vikings engage Ealdorman Byrhtnoth and his troops unless,
that is, they felt that they had a very good chance of success
and thus of gaining the treasure that was their ultimate goal?

Despite their reputation as fierce fighters, in general Vikings showed a remarkable reluctance to engage in battle against organised resistance. They were merciless in their attacks against undefended towns and villages, killing and raping, leaving havoc and destruction everywhere. But they relied heavily on their mobility, particularly on their ability to escape by water, and avoided confrontation with an opposing army wherever possible. At Maldon, as will be shown in a later chapter, they were on an island and they had access to their ships. Byrhtnoth and his army were land-based. There seems to be no obvious explanation for their willingness to do battle other than the belief that they had overwhelming forces sufficient to ensure that the English would quickly sue for peace and buy them off as had happened so often in the past. If their numbers were on the scale that this assumption implies, however, it follows that they constituted a well-organised army. No independently minded group of captains or rag-tag collection of individuals could hope to keep together a considerable force in the single-minded pursuit of a specific aim. The situation required a leader they would all follow, or one who was capable of ensuring that they did. However exaggerated the account of him in the saga tradition may be, there is no doubt that Olaf Tryggvason was such a man. It is important here to consider the sequence of events as reported in the CDE chronicle in the period subsequent to 991. After simply stating of 991 itself that Ipswich was ravaged, that Byrhtnoth was killed at Maldon, and that peace was then bought, three successive annals describe ensuing Viking attacks on England. Excluding the material that relates the succession of bishops and abbots to their respective posts (something with which the *Chronicle* is concerned throughout), the annals read (in version C):

992. The king [Æthelred] and all his counsellors determined that all the ships which were of any use should be gathered at London, and the

king then entrusted the army to Ealdorman Ælfric and Eorl Thored and Bishops Ælfstan and Æscwig. And they should try, if they could, to trap the enemy anywhere on the outside [i.e. on the seaward side of the vikings]. Then the ealdorman Ælfric sent to the enemy and ordered that they be warned, and then on the evening before the day that they were to attack them, he sneaked away from his army during the night to his great shame, and the enemy then escaped, except for the one ship on which the men were killed. Then the enemy met the ships in East Anglia and from London, and they [the English] inflicted great slaughter there and they seized the ship which the ealdorman was on fully weaponed and equipped.

993. In this year Bamburgh [Northumbria] was sacked and a great deal of booty taken from there, and after that the viking army went to the mouth of the Humber and did a great deal of harm there both in Lindsey [Lincolnshire] and in Northumbria. Then a very large defensive force was assembled, and when they were about to go against them, then the commanders of the [English] army instigated a flight. That was Fræna and Godwin and Frythegyst. In this year the king commanded that Ælfgar the son of Ealdorman Ælfric be blinded.

994. In this year Olaf and Swein came to London town on the Nativity of the Virgin Mary [September 8] with ninety-four ships, and they then continued fighting fiercely against the town and also intended to set fire to it, but they [the vikings] there experienced more destruction and evil than they ever thought any citizenry could inflict. But God's holy mother that day showed the citizens her mercy and rescued them from their enemies. The vikings turned away from there and created the greatest destruction that ever any army could do in burning and pillaging and murder both along the seacoast and in Essex and Kent and Sussex and Hampshire. And next they captured horses and rode as far [inland] as they wanted and were continuously creating an indescribable amount of wickedness. Then the king and his counsellors decided that an envoy should be sent to them and promised them tribute and provisions in return for their stopping the pillaging, and they accepted that then. And all the viking army then came to

Hampshire and took up winter quarters there. And people throughout Wessex fed them there, and they were given sixteen thousand pounds. Then the king sent Bishop Ælfheah and Ealdorman Æthelweard to King Olaf, and [English] hostages were left for a time in the ships, and they led Olaf with great honour to Andover. And King Æthelred stood sponsor for [Olaf] at baptism and rewarded him royally, and Olaf promised that he would never come against England again in enmity, and he did just as he promised.

In addition to the information overtly presented here, more can be deduced when this sequence of entries is read between the lines. First, the English failure is attributed to disloyalty on the part of their leaders, which contrasts with what happened in 991 (see Chapter 5), even though when confrontations actually took place, the English defenders were capable of inflicting real damage on the vikings, as in 994 when the Londoners defeated their attackers. Second, the vikings were anxious to avoid a fight where possible, as in 992 when they were forewarned. Having failed to take London, even with their overwhelming numbers, they turned to harrying the less well-protected countryside, but always they remained mobile, by sea or on horseback. It is also apparent that Æthelred was not simply the ineffectual king that the historical tradition suggests. He took retribution for Ealdorman Ælfric's treason by blinding his son, and had an alternative policy against the Vikings when military opposition failed. Offering to act as sponsor to Olaf at his baptism with the promise of rich gifts can be read not simply as appeasement but as a strategy of divide and rule. The opening of the 994 annal makes clear that Olaf and Swein Forkbeard, king of Denmark, were co-leaders of the Viking campaign. But Swein was not included in Æthelred's treaty with Olaf. Swein was already Christian, and is not amongst the named vikings of the treaty's opening clause. Æthelred's tactic of standing as a godfather at the conversion of an opposing leader had a precedent in King Alfred's

conduct towards Guthrum, king of the East Angles, after the
battle of Edington in 878. Æthelred's move, moreover, like
Alfred's, succeeded. Once he had converted to a new faith,
Olaf, the archetypal Viking, left England for ever, returned
to his native land, Norway, and took it by force, aided certainly by English money and perhaps by the English king,
in the last throw of his divide and rule dice. Olaf spent the
last few years of the millennium introducing Christianity
to his new realm, a process that would take longer than
the five years that were left to him before he was killed
by Swein at the end of the century. The fact that the 994
chronicler refers to him as King Olaf shows that he knew
the rest of his story, although it is an anachronistic reference
at this point.

The peace which Æthelred bought in 994 was sealed by a
treaty known to modern scholars as *II Æthelred* (numbered
as part of the sequence of Æthelred's law-codes) which
survives in a manuscript which also contains a copy of the
treaty between Alfred and Guthrum which in some ways
it reflects, although its provisions are much wider. The first
provision of *II Æthelred* states that the English led by Sigeric,
archbishop of Canterbury, and the ealdormen of Wessex
should pay tribute to the Vikings, with the permission of
the king, that the English would supply them with food, and
that if any enemy fleet should attack England, the Vikings
would help to repel them. The first two of these provisions
agree with the *Chronicle* account, but the last is an important
extension of what is said there. Since the only further attack
that might come was by other Vikings, this is a further sign
of the success of Æthelred's divide and rule policy, especially since a number of Viking leaders (including Olaf) are
mentioned by name in the treaty, but significantly Swein,
as stated above, is not and therefore must not have been
party to it.

The strategy of employing Vikings against other Vikings
implied in *II Æthelred* was not new. When Charles the

Simple set up the duchy of Normandy early in the tenth century, one item of the treaty was the agreement that the 'Normans' would guard the French coast against further attack. The second provision of Æthelred's treaty deals with merchant vessels, English and foreign, and is designed to ensure that they should be allowed to trade in peace, unmolested by the Viking army. Five more provisions follow, each one dealing with an aspect of the legal status of men on both the Viking and the English sides and their rights and responsibilities at law. Finally, the total amount paid to the Vikings is specified at twenty-two thousand pounds of gold and silver, rather more than the amount noted in the *Chronicle*, but since Arabic numerals were not introduced to western Europe until long after this date, and all numbers were expressed in Roman script, scribes were notoriously inaccurate in the copying of figures. It is thus just possible that *xvi* was written as *xxi* and later as *xxii*. More plausibly perhaps, it has been recently argued that *II Æthelred* is a treaty which draws together a number of separate earlier agreements made between the archbishop and individual ealdormen and Vikings, and that the sum is a total embracing a number of local arrangements. The figures in the *Chronicle* suggest a steady upward progression as the Vikings realised the strength of their ability to exact tribute: £10,000 in 991, £16,000 in 994, £24,000 in 1002, £36,000 in 1007, and a massive £48,000 in 1012.

If we take the CDE chronicle report at face value, we get a strong impression that the Viking fleet harrying England throughout the period 991–994 was essentially the same one. There is, after all, no specific mention of the arrival of a fleet in 992. Only in 994 are we told that the army stayed in England for the winter, but that does not mean that they did not do so in other years, only that the English were not obliged to provision them if they did. A Welsh chronicle describes Swein son of Harold as engaging in Viking activity on the Isle of Man in 995, which might indicate where Swein was in that year, although since both Swein and Harold are common Norse names, it is impossible to be sure that the reference is to Swein Forkbeard. Certainly Swein returned to Denmark in 995 to protect his position there. That Olaf and Swein were together in England in 994 is beyond doubt, but that in itself does not help solve the question of whether either or both of them was in the country before that, leading the army that is described in 994, or whether they came together for the first time in that year. The very precise wording of the CDE chronicle, 'in this year Olaf and Swein came to London town on the Nativity of the Virgin Mary', may not be as significant as was once supposed, but may derive from the fact that the chronicler compiled his account in London and had intimate details of that particular attack. Viking sources describe Olaf as raiding on the continent, then in southern England, and then in the north, which is consistent with natural geographic progression, and the *Chronicle* certainly reports raids in the north in 993. It may be that specific leaders came and went, as indeed individual vessels or groups of ships, but we are surely dealing throughout this period with a large body of ships and men, under a strong leadership, who recognised the possibility of exploiting the wealth of England while the country's leaders were in disarray. With regard to the battle of Maldon, the presence of Olaf is possible, but unproven, and the historical record suggests other potential leaders. The *Chronicle of chronicles*, for example, the work of a monk from Worcester known as John of Worcester (early twelfth century), names two Viking leaders at the battle, Justin and Guthmund. Nothing is known about the latter, but the former was an uncle of Olaf and might perhaps have been fighting alongside him. As the title of John's work suggests, his is a compilation of earlier chronicles, not all of which survive, and where he adds information that cannot be traced to a known source, it is possible that he had access to a chronicle now lost. In this case, however, he may have taken the names from *II Æthelred*, and his use of them is therefore suspect. In *II Æthelred*, the Viking leaders named as parties to the truce are Olaf, Justin and Guthmund. It is perhaps surprising that John should name two of these men but not Olaf if he was indeed drawing on *II Æthelred*, but the treaty is in English and represents Olaf as Anlaf, a form of the name that a Latin chronicler working 150 years later may not have understood. Justin and Guthmund are more obviously names, while both *an* and *laf* are Old English words and hence susceptible to misconstruction. Nevertheless, John's account was followed by two other twelfth-century chroniclers, Symeon of Durham and the author of the *Liber Eliensis*. Symeon's work is wholly derived from John's, and provides no independent source, but the *Liber Eliensis* or 'Book of Ely' must be considered more fully, since the Ely monastery benefited greatly from Byrhtnoth's will and the ealdorman himself is buried there. No doubt traditions concerning him survived orally, and perhaps also in written form, but there is no concrete evidence that the Ely source offers an independent witness to the identity of the leaders at Maldon.

There is more substantive evidence for Swein being the leader on the Viking side at Maldon rather than any of the other possible contenders. Not only is it known that he was in England three years later and that he remained a constant threat to the English from then on, but he was in the best position to muster sufficient troops for the battle, though there is no surviving record of his presence at the scene. All versions of the *Chronicle* report that Ipswich was sacked before the encounter, and it is very probable that the other towns mentioned in chronicle A, Folkestone and Sandwich, had been raided before that. If the fleet was not satisfied with the booty that it had obtained in the campaign before Maldon but then went on to lay siege to another town, and was willing to risk a confrontation with Byrhtnoth's forces in the hope of gaining more tribute, its size must have been formidable indeed. More tellingly, perhaps, after the battle, during which sources indicate that many Vikings died or were too grievously wounded to be fit for further action, the remnant of the Viking army still posed a sufficient threat for the English to be obliged to buy them off for a sum stated in all versions of the *Chronicle* as ten thousand pounds of silver. The CDE chronicle report that sixteen thousand pounds of silver was paid in tribute to the Vikings in 994, as well as provision for the winter, suggesting that the armies in 991 and 994 were of the same magnitude. Even after the battle of Maldon then, the Viking army must still have been very large indeed. The CDE chronicle reports that ninety-four ships descended on London in 994, and though some of the ships and many of the men in them may have been lost before tribute was paid, and although numbers may not be exact, nonetheless what the chronicler suggests is that the Viking fleet and its army was of a formidable size. Given that all the sources (except the twelfth-century *Liber Eliensis*) maintain that there was huge slaughter at the battle of Maldon, the scale of the Viking army at the outset must have been of the same order as that which attacked London three years later. It is not unreasonable, therefore, to accept the A version account that the fleet which attacked Folkestone, Ipswich and Maldon consisted of some ninety-three ships.

Both estimates of the numbers of ships involved in these encounters, ninety-three according to A at Maldon and ninety-four according to CDE at London, have to be seen as a rough guide, indicative of the size of the force rather than a precise count. We do know, however, that in 994, both Swein and Olaf were present at the attack, and we know from literary sources that Olaf's Long Serpent had sixty-eight oars, which means that together with the helmsman, Olaf himself, and perhaps some of his closest lieutenants, the ship's complement was over seventy. On the evidence of Hedeby 1 and Roskilde 6, Swein probably had as big a

boat as Olaf's at least, which means that certainly two of
whatever ships there were in the Thames in 994 contained
150 men between them. Most of the warships would have
been much smaller, of course, but Skuldelev 5 suggests that
even they are likely to have held around thirty men. Even if
it is assumed that ninety-four ships is an overestimate, there
is little doubt that the force that attacked London was numbered in thousands, perhaps as many as 3,000 or substantially
more. The same can be said of Maldon, although it needs
to be pointed out that in a land battle away from the ships,
as at Maldon, the number of Vikings involved would be
reduced by the number needed to guard the boats. The fight
described in the *Anglo-Saxon Chronicle* entry for 897, where
nine of Alfred's new longships took on six Viking ships,
shows that a significant number of raiders was left with
the boats while land raids were taking place. Nonetheless,
there can be little doubt that thousands of Vikings were
present at Maldon in 991, even though only a proportion
of them took part in the battle. Assembling that number of
men, and organising and controlling both them and their
ships took someone of considerable power and authority.
Even the charismatic figure of Olaf Tryggvason is unlikely
to have been able to raise that number of troops, although
they might well follow him once they were assembled in a
battle situation. Only Swein, with the resources of Denmark
behind him, could have mounted such an army. Precisely
what his resources were is a matter of debate. No Danish
legal material exists before the end of the eleventh century,
but law codes do survive from Norway and Sweden, and it
is reasonable to suppose that the situation in Denmark may
have been similar. The tenth-century Norwegian Gulating
Code, the most important of these survivals, specifies the
obligation of each region to supply, maintain and man a
ship for the defence of the realm, this duty being overseen
by the king's representative. The manner in which the small
warship Skuldelev 5, described in the last chapter, was built

and maintained suggests an effort on the part of its owners
to economise in the use of materials and to ensure the
long life of the vessel, thus reducing the burden on the
population of supplying a new ship. Since Skuldelev 5 is a
Danish ship, it would appear that laws approximating to the
Gulating Code applied in Denmark too. Skuldelev 5 was
built around 1030, a generation after Swein's death, and it
might seem to be too late to supply convincing evidence of
conditions obtaining in the 990s, especially since no com-
parable ship survives from the late tenth century. But in
the time of Swein's father, Denmark was sufficiently well
organised militarily to allow for the building of elaborate
road and bridge works, and for the construction of army
training camps such as that at Jellinge – and such works
could not have been produced without a competent system
of military obligation being enforced. If Harold Bluetooth
was able to impose the duty of building such works on the
populace, his son would have inherited a coherent defence
capability, and the likelihood that he extended it into boat
building and manning is great. With such an organisation,
the assembling of a fleet of the size that attacked London
in 994, and which fought the battle of Maldon three years
earlier, would not be an impossible enterprise.

The final piece of evidence that offers modern historians
an indication that Swein himself was at Maldon comes from
an unlikely source, a legal document dated, by reference to
its witness list, between 995 and 999. In it, King Æthelred
confirmed the will of a minor nobleman of Essex known
as Æthelric of Bocking (on Osea Island, see page 131). The
document makes clear that confirmation was in jeopardy
because Æthelric had been involved, like so many members of the aristocracy of the time, in a plot to receive
Swein in Essex when he first came there with a fleet 'many
years before Æthelric died'. The confirmation was made in
response to the plea of Æthelric's widow Leofwynn, but the
significance for the activities of Swein lies in a single word

ærest 'first', the intention of the plotters being to receive him when Swein *first* came to Essex. After 994 there is no further mention of Swein in England until 1003 (in 999/1000 he was in Norway re-establishing his claim to the throne by killing Olaf), and if the use of *first* is literal, as the context suggests, then Swein brought a fleet to England, where many were prepared to receive him, *before* any mention in the *Chronicle* of the fleet that attacked Essex in 994 and that he and Olaf led. This offers as clear confirmation as we are likely to get that Swein was in Essex in 991.

4

The English Response

In the last decade of the ninth century, King Alfred, as noted above, ordered a new design of English ship to defend his shores against Viking attacks. It is clear from the *Anglo-Saxon Chronicle* account of that period that the English navy was well organised and successful against the relatively small-scale invasions that were prevalent at that time. In the annal for 911, for example, the *Chronicle* states that Edward the Elder gathered 100 ships against a

Northumbrian insurrection and an invasion of Mercia. In
934 Æthelstan's movement against Scotland was both by
land and by sea. Clearly in these three successive reigns, the
English naval force was supreme. A poem on King Edgar's
death recorded in the E chronicle states that no foreign fleet
was able to invade during his reign. But English command
of the seas faded during the reign of his son Æthelred, a fact
indicated by the resumption of Viking raids shortly after he
succeeded in 978. It is significant that against the large-scale
attack of 992 the king summoned all the ships 'which were
of any use', implying that the navy had fallen into disrepair.
Perhaps these were in fact the very ships that were in use
in Edgar's day, shipbuilding having lapsed since his death in
975, during a period when England lacked strong central
government. Ships built before the 970s, however, would
have been of little use by 992. In the new century Æthelred
realised how disastrous the policy of allowing the navy to
deteriorate had been and had instituted new laws by 1008:
every 300 hides should provide a warship and every ten hides
a skeith. A hide was sufficient land to support an extended
family including slaves and retainers (the Old English word
for the members of a household was *hiwan*, which is related
to *hid* 'hide'), which in practice meant anything from 60 to
120 acres, depending on the productivity of the land, but
which in the pre-Conquest period was usually closer to the
upper end of that scale.

Laws relating to the provision of a national army were
already in place in the tenth century. Those who held land
by charter from the king were obliged in time of need to
provide one armed man for every five hides of land held,
and were expected to serve the king personally with their
immediate entourage. As a group, these men constituted
what is known as the 'select *fyrd*', fyrd being the Old English
word for a national army of defence. This was the first of
what historians call the three 'common burdens' on land-
holding, the other two being bridge building and work on

the building and manning of the forts. The maintenance of bridges was a necessary part of keeping the country in a state of preparation for war, as armies needed to cross rivers speedily and with ease. Under Alfred and Edward the Elder, the common burdens had become statutory obligations for landholders, but peace led to the abandonment of the national army. Instead, as power passed to the regions, the ealdormen were responsible to the king for leading the men of their individual shires in the defence of their own region, and when they fought alongside one another in a more major engagement, with the king or his appointed leader at their head (as is described in the *Anglo-Saxon Chronicle* entry for 992, quoted in the last chapter), the troops were still mustered by shires (and within shires, it would seem, by hundreds) and fought under the standard of their own ealdorman. In all cases, the national army or the more local one might be supplemented by local levies of untrained and poorly armed peasants from the region, the so-called 'great *fyrd*'. In the latter part of Æthelred's reign when treason and disloyalty were at a height, the king found that there were times when the ealdormen refused to raise their levies, as the *Chronicle* reports in 1009, and in 1016 large fines had to be threatened against those who refused to raise any troops. In that year, the levies that were raised refused to fight unless the king was with them. Yet when they all came together, as the chronicler sourly remarks, 'it all came to nothing'. All of this goes to prove the growing strength of the nobility in Æthelred's time, and the corresponding decline in the authority of the crown.

The towns fared no better under Æthelred. By the late tenth century, the urbanisation of England which had begun under King Alfred had gathered momentum, towns had grown both in size and importance, and many, including some which had developed in Viking-held areas, had become European and international ports. The archaeology of York, now displayed at the Jorvik Centre in the city, shows

clearly that the town was involved in Viking trade with all
corners of the known world. London was the largest town
in the country because of the great wealth that merchants
brought to the city. Ipswich in East Anglia was a close rival.
It has been calculated that by the end of the century at
least five towns in England had more than 5,000 inhabitants (York, Lincoln, Winchester, Stamford and Chester) and
London may have had as many as 10,000. There were many
other towns, moreover, especially ports like Ipswich and
Southampton, which were not far short of these in size.
But like the navy and the army, the defence of the towns
had deteriorated since the early years of the century. The
long period of peace under Edgar meant that the practice
of maintaining town walls and a permanent garrison had
been abandoned, and walls had even been breached and
dykes filled in to allow for tenth-century urban expansion.
This made civic communities extremely vulnerable to a
fresh wave of attacks.

The Viking assault upon London in 994 failed in all probability because the walls had been adequately maintained,
and there were very large numbers of citizens to rain down
missiles and fire bolts onto the Viking ships on the Thames.
London was confined to the north bank of the river at that
period (and for many years after that), but the 991 raids that
preceded the battle of Maldon were against much smaller
towns with populations quite unable to withstand thousands of well-armed men. The *Anglo-Saxon Chronicle* for
991 survives in two versions. The relevant passage in CDE
states simply that:

> In this year Ipswich was sacked, and very soon after that Ealdorman
> Byrhtnoth was killed at Maldon. In that year the vikings were first paid
> tribute because of the great destruction that they were making along
> the coast. It consisted of ten thousand pounds. Archbishop Sigeric
> first gave that advice.

The A version has a fuller account of the attack:

> In this year Olaf came with ninety-three ships to Folkestone and they
> raided all around it. And then he went from there to Sandwich, and so
> from there to Ipswich and overran all around that, and so to Maldon.
> And Ealdorman Byrhtnoth came against them there with his levies
> and fought against them, and they killed the ealdorman there and had
> control of the battlefield. And afterwards peace was made with them,
> and the king stood sponsor to him at baptism, through the advice of
> Sigeric bishop of Canterbury and Ælfheah bishop of Winchester.

As was noted in the last chapter, the A version is entered
by mistake under 993, and the information in the last sentence belongs to the year 994 when peace was made with
Olaf. But this does not mean that all of A's extra material
should be discounted. There is no reason for the chronicler
to invent the sacking of Folkestone and Sandwich. The most
reasonable explanation for the confusion of the entry in
A (note the switch between *he* and *they/them* and back
again, and the dislocation of annal date) is that the material was received piecemeal from different sources, and was
imperfectly put together. There is good evidence to suggest that the A chronicle was written at Winchester, and it
had certainly been transferred to Canterbury by 1006. If it
was indeed written in a major centre like Winchester, with
Canterbury connections, the additional information might
well have come from a Canterbury source, and an inform-
ant at Canterbury was in an excellent position to know in
detail about events in Kent.

Folkestone was a small settlement in 991, perhaps no
more than a group of buildings surrounding a seventh-
century minster church, but charter evidence suggests that
the foundation derived wealth from land in 991, and was
therefore rich in material goods. It was probably protected
by no more than a wooden stockade, and the town's few
hundred inhabitants were hardly in a position to withstand a

large-scale attack. It is interesting to note that the chronicler
writes of the whole of the region around Folkestone being
raided. The town was of strategic significance in that it lay
at the eastern end of an ancient trackway that ran along
the highest point of the Weald across to Ilchester where
it joined a Roman road to Exeter in the west. It was a
principal highway through the dense forest of the Weald,
and a number of other minsters within a five-mile radius of
Folkestone itself were brought, through the town's capture,
within easy reach of raiding parties from the Viking ships.
A large fleet would have rich pickings in the area and good
supplies of provisions, without having to engage any serious
military opposition.

The situation at Sandwich was quite different. Before the
River Stour began to silt up, it was wide and deep enough
to accommodate large ships, and the harbour at Sandwich
was thus an important one in the later tenth century and
for the next hundred years. The town had been sacked by
the Vikings in 851, and in 1006 a fleet led by Swein from
Denmark attacked Sandwich again and, according to the
Chronicle, 'ravaged, burned and killed wherever they went'.
Ships of the new English fleet which Æthelred had ordered
in 1008 were brought together for the first time at that
town in 1009. In short, this was a major port which acted
as a deep-sea outlet for London – indeed it was probably
the principal port of the earlier kingdom of Kent, when
London was part of Essex – and it was also a significant
access point for inland Kent. In particular, it served as both
port and first line of defence for Canterbury, just twelve
miles away by Roman road and only a little further by
water along the Stour. Although Canterbury had walled,
Roman defences, its susceptibility to capture became apparent in 1011 when it was sacked (according to the *Chronicle*
by the treachery of the abbot of the nearby St Augustine's
monastery) and the archbishop, Ælfheah, taken prisoner.
When he refused to allow himself to be ransomed, he was

pelted with animal bones (a traditional Viking form of punishment) until finally killed by a single blow from an axe to the head. He was buried at the church of St Paul's in London, but in 1023 was translated to Canterbury where he became Canterbury's most important martyr up to the time of Thomas Becket. In the year of the martyrdom, 1012 according to the *Chronicle* account, the men of forty-five of the Viking ships swore allegiance to Æthelred, encouraging the reader to conclude that the killing of the archbishop was instrumental in their changing sides, as hinted by one Latin source. Sandwich too was an important town in its own right, with its own mint and defences, although as with all towns without Roman foundations, its fortifications were almost certainly of wood. Though not mentioned by name in Domesday because it then belonged to the monastery of Christchurch at Canterbury, it may be presumed that it had up to a thousand inhabitants. The present-day layout of the town still follows the pattern of the Anglo-Saxon streets, with wide roads running inland away from the quayside, although the wooden houses of the period have disappeared without trace.

Of the four towns mentioned in the A chronicle account, Ipswich was by far the largest. Recent archaeological excavations have shown that it was a major commercial town, with defences that had been built, ironically, by the Danes themselves in the early tenth century when they ruled East Anglia. The fortunes of the town derived originally from pottery, but by the end of the tenth century it had diversified into a variety of manufacturing industries, and it was a flourishing port with many wealthy merchants and burgesses in 991 living in two-story buildings. Its sack was a significant blow to the East Anglian economy. In the Domesday survey, it is reported that 538 burgesses were tenants of the king, which suggests a late-tenth-century population of at least 4,000. It had flourished in the ninth century when other ports in the south were badly affected by Viking disruption of trade, because East Anglia from the middle of the century was ruled by Viking settlers and therefore escaped further predation. In the tenth century, when trade across the North Sea became easier, it continued to expand first through trade with Scandinavia with which there were historical links, and later with the Rhineland and Normandy as the English economy became increasingly dependent upon sheep exports, both of meat and more importantly of wool. The huge payments in tribute made by the English to the Vikings from 991 onwards can be explained only by England having a large balance of payments surplus throughout those years, and that surplus arose mainly through the export of wool. Three ports were instrumental in shipping the great output of the wool industry of East Anglia to the continent: London, Norwich and Ipswich. London and Norwich were among the biggest and wealthiest towns in late-tenth-century England, and Ipswich was not far behind them. Given its connections with Scandinavia, it is not surprising that men of the Viking fleet were well aware of the significance of Ipswich, and of the value which would accrue from a successful raid on the town. But the cost of the attack to Ipswich is hard to comprehend. As with all such towns in the Anglo-Saxon period, the predominant building material was wood. Few buildings would have survived the conflagration which regularly followed a major Viking raid. The majority of the inhabitants would have had little opportunity to flee, and there is no report of significant resistance. The *Chronicle* account of the attack on Southampton in 980, a town of similar size and wealth, indicates that most of the population were either taken prisoner or killed, and it is difficult to be sure which would have seemed preferable to the unfortunate inhabitants of the town.

After Ipswich, the fleet moved into Essex and threatened Maldon. The precise boundaries of Essex in the tenth century are now uncertain, but in the early Anglo-Saxon period, the kingdom of the East Saxons was a major power, one of the seven in the Heptarchy discussed by Bede (died 735) which shared the overlordship of England in turn. The kingdom was one of the first to have a bishop, at St Paul's in its capital of London in 604, a development deriving from pressure by the kingdom of Kent where English Christianity was first established in 597. At the time of the bishop's appointment, Essex extended much further west than the present county, and during the seventh century London grew to be an important trading centre. Its success attracted the adverse attention, however, of larger and more powerful neighbours. By the end of the eighth century, Mercia had taken the western half of Essex, including London, and created a sub-kingdom of Middle Saxons (Middlesex) under its own control as a species of buffer zone. As Mercian dominance of England diminished during the early part of the ninth century and that of Wessex grew, Alfred's grandfather, King Egbert, took over the kingdom of Essex in 825 and made it a West Saxon dependency, and, as had happened to Kent at a slightly earlier date, it rapidly declined to a West Saxon ealdordom. With the Viking invasions of the second half of the ninth century Wessex lost control of Essex itself, and although King Alfred took possession of London in 880, his agreement with the East Anglian king Guthrum after the latter's defeat in 878, conceded that the rest of Essex should remain under Viking control. It was not until the military successes of Edward the Elder in the tenth century that Essex was retaken and the Wessex ealdormanry re-established. Nevertheless, it would seem that the ealdormen of Essex in the tenth century had control of a much larger area than that comprised by the county today, including within their domain present-day Essex, Middlesex and the eastern half of Hertfordshire. Leofsige, Byrhtnoth's successor as ealdorman, appears to have governed Oxfordshire and Buckinghamshire as well.

Away from its coastline, much of Essex was very heavily wooded, densely forested with oak, ash, maple, hazel, hornbeam and elm. Beech, the staple provider of mast for feeding pigs, appears to have been less common. There were only two towns, the bigger being Colchester, an old Roman site the stone walls of which had been renovated by King Edward early in the tenth century. The strength of its defences coupled with the fact that it was sufficiently far inland up the river Colne to make it difficult to access, might account for the decision of the large Viking fleet involved in the 991 attack to move further down the Essex coast in search of another, easier, target. It is noticeable that none of the towns in the course of this raid, Folkestone, Sandwich and Ipswich, are known to have had stone fortifications. Ipswich had been the best fortified of the three, but the growth of the town in the tenth century may mean that the walls had been removed in places to allow for expansion of the population.

Maldon was the second largest town in Essex after Colchester. In 1086 it had a house owned by the king with pasture for 100 sheep, and 180 burgesses each with a house held from the crown, together with eighteen 'wasted', i.e. empty, houses. Calculations based on Domesday Book suggest that Colchester had a population in 1066 of at least 2,000, and there is no reason to suppose that this would be less in 991. Maldon, by contrast, probably had fewer than 1,000, including women and children, a number far short of the force required to withstand an attack by three times as many armed men for long, even if its defences were intact, but perhaps enough to hold out under siege until the town could be relieved by regular English troops. We have no means of knowing if the defences were adequate, but Maldon occupies an easily defended site, on a bluff overlooking a bend in the river where the Blackwater narrows when approached from the sea. Although the river is still tidal at that point and sufficiently deep for the Viking boats to have sailed past the town, it is narrow enough for damage with missiles and firebrands to be done from the town walls to ships passing below (see Plates 41 and 42). Whatever the reason, the Vikings either decided not to storm the town or failed in their attempt to do so. Instead, they camped on Northey Island, a mile downstream, an island which is connected to the south bank of the river by an ancient Roman causeway accessible only at low tide (see Plates 44, 45 and 46). It was there that they were confronted by Ealdorman Byrhtnoth and his English troops.

Close examination of the *Chronicle* accounts of the events of the year 991 shows that the prime concern of the CDE version is that Byrhtnoth was killed very soon after Ipswich was sacked, and even the A version with its greater detail of the accompanying events devotes a large part of the entry to a report of Byrhtnoth's stand against the enemy and the fact that he died at their hands. The death of an ealdorman was highly significant in Anglo-Saxon England, and the clear implication of the entry of 991 is that it led to the payment of tribute to the Danes for the first time. But Byrhtnoth in 991 was not just one of a number of ealdormen. He was the most senior active ealdorman of the time. We know nothing of his father except that, according to one source, his name was Byrhthelm, but there is documentary evidence that an ealdorman by the name of Byrhtferth, probably ealdorman of Essex, signed charters during 955 and 956. It was the practice amongst noble families to use the same name element from one generation to the next. King Edward the Elder, for example, whose name in Old English is *Eadweard*, has a son *Eadmund* ('Edmund') and a grandson *Eadgar* ('Edgar'). It was also usual in the tenth century for governorship of the regions to pass either from father to son or, at least, to another member of a closely related family group. It is likely then that Byrhtnoth succeeded either an older brother or – more probably – an uncle as ealdorman of Essex in 956. Prior to this time he had witnessed charters as a thegn. His appointment to the rank of ealdorman was made during the short reign of King Eadwig, Edgar's elder brother (reigned

955–959), but his designation as thegn prior to his appointment might suggest that he was already in line for promo-
tion under King Eadred who died in 955. The fact that he
signed charters as ealdorman from as early as 956 shows both
that he was extremely experienced by 991 and that he was
of advanced years for a man at that period. An ealdorman
who ruled a major province for thirty-five years – more
than the reign of most kings – must have lived much longer
than was the norm at that time.

The evidence suggests that he was probably married twice,
the second marriage being to Ælfflæd, a daughter of Ælfgar,
an earlier ealdorman of Essex who died in 951. Records
at Ely show that Byrhtnoth had a daughter of his own,
Leofflæd, but she seems not to have been by Ælfflæd even
though the two share the name element -flæd. There is a
great paucity of female name elements in Anglo-Saxon and
–flæd is among the most common. Leofflæd did not receive
any of the property which Ælfgar bequeathed to the heirs
of Byrhtnoth and Ælfflæd, nor did any of Leofflæd's four
children or her grandson. She may, of course, have been a
daughter of Byrhtnoth by a concubine, although her own
high status is suggested by the fact that her will was addressed
to King Cnut and Queen Emma. Byrhtnoth's father-in-law,
Ælfgar, had two daughters, Ælfflæd being the younger. The
elder, Æthelflæd, was the second wife of King Edmund, King
Æthelred's grandfather, and so, by a rather circuitous route,
Byrhtnoth can be shown to be related to each of the kings
he served during his long career. This is consistent with the
fact that all the principal members of the aristocracy were
related to each other in some way, something that helped
to bind the country together even though its constituent
parts were in many respects self-governing. He had other
noble connections: Ælfwine, who fought alongside him at
Maldon, is reported as referring to him as his kinsman, and
Ælfwine was a grandson of Ealdorman Ealhhelm of Mercia
(died 951). It has also been suggested that Byrhtnoth was a

great grandson of the Ætheling Beornnoth or Beorhtnoth (Ætheling being the Anglo-Saxon term for a prince of royal blood) who died in 905 in the insurrection against King Edward the Elder, but there is no proof for the proposition beyond the similarity of names. Had he been descended from the Ætheling, his family would have belonged to the old Mercian royal house before its last legitimate king, Burgred, was expelled by the Danish army in 874. He may, however, have had very different connections. Anglo-Saxon kings, like kings of all ages, married for political reasons rather than emotional ones. Ælfgar's elder daughter was married to King Edmund. The marriage helped ensure that the king's father-in-law remained faithful while ruling an important area north of the Thames, and it is possible that the king might have engineered the marriage of Ælfgar's younger daughter to a junior member of his household or to a son of a cadet branch of the West Saxon royal house. The Essex ealdordom would then pass from Ælfgar, who was without a male heir, to his son-in-law's family, tying it ever more closely to Wessex. It is apparent from the fact that Ælfgar mentions Byrhtnoth as his daughter's husband in his will that the marriage had taken place before 951, forty years before the battle in 991. If it is assumed that Byrhtnoth had indeed been married previously, he must have been around twenty when he married Ælfflæd, and that would make him at least sixty when he died. Few of his contemporaries could have taken part in a major battle at that age, let alone lived long enough to participate in it. Written accounts of the battle suggest that he was unusually old when it took place, but the fact that he did in fact take part in it suggests that he was a man of unusual vigour for his years. We know nothing of his appearance except that he was exceptionally tall and that in 991 he had white hair – hardly surprising given his age.

Byrhtnoth's power did not derive solely from his family and their connections; it also lay in the land that he had inherited and acquired, and in the strength of his personality.

That he inherited land is shown by the fact that when he married before 951 he was already in a position to give his bride the rich manor of Rettenden, valued in Domesday Book at 95 shillings, which she in turn gave to Ely in her will. He was closely allied, moreover, to the family of the ealdormen of East Anglia, and in the second quarter of the tenth century, the most powerful man in England after the king was Æthelstan, ealdorman of East Anglia from 932 to 957. This period included the reigns of King Æthelstan (died 939), Edmund (died 946), and the sickly Eadred (died 959). During these turbulent times with short reigns culminating in the succession of a monarch who was often incapable of running the country, Ealdorman Æthelstan's power progressively extended beyond the boundaries of his East Anglian ealdordom. By the end of the tenth century, his reputation was such that he was known as Æthelstan Half-King, though just how early this by-name was used is impossible to say. He had taken over his ealdordom at a time when it had been newly won back from Danish rule, and his court was so important that King Edmund's younger son Edgar was fostered there. Edgar came to the English throne in 959, and he appears to have remained close to two boyhood friends, Æthelwine, a younger son of Æthelstan Half-King who inherited his father's ealdordom in succession to another brother in 962, and Byrhtnoth of Essex, who also grew up at the Half-King's court. At the same time Edgar remained very close to his tutor, a man called Æthelwold who presumably tutored him at the Half-King's court and who was therefore linked both to Ealdorman Æthelwine and to Byrhtnoth. When Edgar became king of England in 959, still under the tutelage of Æthelwold who by then was abbot of Abingdon, he began a reform of the monastic order which had far-reaching consequences in the organisation of the Church and in the economics (and ultimately the politics) of the realm. What has come to be known as the Benedictine reform movement, which began on the continent during the first half of the tenth century and which was centred upon a return to strict observance of the monastic life by monks and nuns following the Benedictine rule, was spread to England by three clerics: Dunstan, who was appointed archbishop of Canterbury in the first year of Edgar's reign; Oswald who was appointed bishop of Worcester two years later in 961 and who held that see in plurality with the archbishopric of York from 971; and Æthelwold, whom Edgar made bishop of Winchester in 963 – Winchester being the old capital of Wessex and still the seat of royal government. Under the auspices of these three, old monasteries were revived and many new ones created, with the result that monastic life everywhere south of the Humber was revitalised, and learning in the vernacular spread throughout the kingdom. Hundreds of books survive from this period, many in English as well as in Latin, and it is no exaggeration to say that the considerable wealth of information that survives on the history of this period, including the most important copies of the *Anglo-Saxon Chronicle*, derives mainly from writings of this period. But this spiritual and intellectual improvement in the life of the nation came at a price. The development of the monasteries could only be achieved with substantial grants of land, and, apart from the king, the largest donors were the ealdormen Æthelwine and Byrhtnoth.

On the death of Edgar in 975, Æthelwine and Byrhtnoth were reported by monastic chronicles as being the loudest voices in favour of the succession of Edgar's elder son Edward (the Martyr) and of the maintenance of the ecclesiastical policies of Edgar's reign. With the murder of Edward in 978, Edgar's younger son Æthelred came to the throne, and Byrhtnoth and Æthelwine lost some of their influence at court in favour of a faction led by Ealdorman Ælfhere of central Mercia. The church lost much of its power and a good deal of the wealth that it had acquired under Edgar. It is not surprising, then, to find monastic writers for many

generations favourable to Byrhtnoth, and we probably owe
the survival of most of the information that we have on both
him and the battle of Maldon to his prestige in ecclesiastical
circles. There is good reason too for ascribing the survival of
the heroic poem known as *The Battle of Maldon*, to which
we owe all the details of the battle, to the desire to preserve
Byrhtnoth's memory in the monastic environment in which
it was almost certainly copied and preserved. But Ælfhere
died in 983, and from then until 991 it was Æthelwine and
Byrhtnoth who signed first and second in the witness lists of
ealdormen to the king's charters, showing that they had the
primary position and greatest influence at court. Together
with the king and the archbishops, they were the greatest
men in England.

Surviving records of Byrhtnoth's property show it to be
so extensive that they made him one of the richest men in
the kingdom, and it is certain that not all his possessions are
yet known. Although his own will does not survive, that of
his wife Ælfflæd does, and it lists many of the estates that
she inherited from him. The will of her sister, the widow of
King Edmund, is also extant and that lists many properties
given to Byrhtnoth, as does the will of his father-in-law
Ælfgar. But the most important source of our knowledge
is the *Liber Eliensis* which lists thirteen manors which he
bequeathed to the monastery at Ely as well as others which
reverted to them on the death of his widow Ælfflæd. His
daughter Leofflæd and her children also bequeathed land
to Ely which presumably came to them from Byrhtnoth.
The wealth of the family persisted through many generations. The widow of his great-grandson Thurstan still had
very substantial land holdings in 1066, as Domesday Book
makes clear. Although Ely was his most favoured religious
house, many other monasteries benefited from his will,
among them Mersea in his own county of Essex, Ramsey
which was founded by Bishop Oswald and endowed by
Ealdorman Æthelwine, Abingdon, an old abbey re-founded

by Bishop Æthelwold, and Christchurch Canterbury, the seat of Dunstan. Much of his property would have been in Essex, but the records show that he also had estates in East Anglia, Cambridgeshire, Oxfordshire, Buckinghamshire, Northamptonshire and even as far west as Worcestershire. His great wealth no doubt added to and was part of his prestige within the governing classes of England. It would also have increased his power in terms of the number of men at his command. Byrhtnoth's domain of Essex was, as was suggested above, much wider than the present county, extending far to the west of the present borders. The poet of *The Battle of Maldon* includes a Northumbrian hostage among Byrhtnoth's entourage and, if the report provides an independent witness, the *Liber Eliensis* suggests that he controlled Northumbria. This too may be a significant indication of the extent of his power. The taking of hostages to ensure the good behaviour of the hostage's family and friends was a common practice, and the southern kings in later tenth-century England needed to be on their guard constantly against Northumbrian disaffection. In fact, no insurrection is reported between 954 and the early years of the eleventh century, but this may derive from the fact that Northumbria was tightly controlled. If the poet's report and the references in the *Liber Eliensis* are accurate, it would appear that Byrhtnoth had some responsibility for the north, which, given his position within the Anglo-Saxon hierarchy, would not be altogether surprising. In 991, moreover, Ealdorman Æthelwine was seriously ill (he died in April of the following year), and his incapacity left Byrhtnoth in the position of the principal ealdorman of the realm. In brief, in taking an army to battle against the Vikings at Maldon, he was not just governor of Essex defending his own county, but the king's viceroy.

Sandwich is sixty miles from London and a further forty miles from Colchester, near the eastern border with Suffolk. If Byrhtnoth was anywhere in Essex when Sandwich was attacked, he would have known about it within a matter of hours. By the time the Vikings could reach Ipswich via the North Sea (about sixty nautical miles, or 100 kilometres), they would have sailed for no less than six hours and probably for nearer a full day, assuming that they sailed at the speed of the slowest ship in the fleet and thus at a maximum of ten knots. Leaving in the morning, they could not have expected to arrive before nightfall, and would hardly have embarked on a raid as night was beginning to fall. The attack on Ipswich thus could not in all probability have taken place until at least two days after the assault on Sandwich. This period would have been sufficient to allow Byrhtnoth to send out a call to arms, but was certainly not long enough for his troops to have assembled, and he may not furthermore have been able to track the direction taken by the Vikings while they were on the open sea. Even though Ipswich was in the East Anglian ealdordom, Byrhtnoth would no doubt have felt that, with Æthelwine ill, he was responsible for its defence, and he would in any case have felt the consequences of such an attack deeply since he possessed at least four manors within a twelve-mile radius of the town, and probably, since this was the pattern with market towns, a house within the borough itself. Without some prior knowledge of the target of the attack, he would not have been able to muster his troops in an appropriate place to mount a defence, and hence Ipswich was left to its fate. The sack of such a major settlement, however, would have occupied the Vikings for a full day, and they may have spent more time in loading their booty onto their ships. To regroup and sail off in search of another target would have taken their commanders an even longer period of time. Throughout this interval, Byrhtnoth was no doubt engaged in assembling troops. He was clearly able to assemble the select fyrd of the whole of his domain of 'greater Essex', and perhaps drew some experienced troops from neighbouring counties. Since it appears that the Vikings sailed along the Essex coast to Maldon, his scouts would have undoubtedly been able to track their progress. They first passed south around the Naze, and since they then sailed west into the Blackwater estuary, they would have passed the estuary of the River Colne on which Colchester lies some eight or nine miles from the sea. They chose, it seems, to ignore Colchester as noted above, and many reasons may be adduced to account for this decision. It is highly unlikely that they did not know of the town's existence, since they appear to have had very detailed information on coastal towns in eastern and southern England, but they may also have known that it was defended by Roman stone walls, and perhaps suspected that it would be garrisoned by Byrhtnoth by the time that they got there. Their decision to turn into the Blackwater and threaten Maldon would have been known to Byrhtnoth, however, almost as soon as that choice was made.

A fleet that was large enough to do the damage that was done in 991, and which was still big enough to be in a position to demand a significant amount of tribute even after the battle (see Chapter 3), would have taken some time to sail up the river and beach on Northey Island. The camp that the Vikings established on the island suggests that they paused to take stock of the situation, and determined not to attack the town immediately, either because the borough was too well defended or because Byrhtnoth was already there. The town was well protected on the side abutting the river by its slightly raised position, and once the Vikings had chosen to beach on the island, they were at a distance of around a mile from the town. Their landing on an island – if we accept the evidence of the introduction to the poem *The Battle of Maldon* (and there is no good reason to doubt its accuracy, as will be shown in the next chapter) – suggests that they planned a land attack, and for that they would be reliant on the tides. The island is connected to the mainland by a causeway that had been in existence since at least Roman times, and so an attack would need to be carefully timed, as the causeway is passable only at low tide. The assault would also have to be quickly accomplished, in order to allow the invaders time to return to their ships before the incoming tide left them stranded and exposed. These two factors might have suggested to a competent Viking commander that although Northey Island offered a secure harbour for his ships while he mounted his attack on the town, he would need to choose his moment very precisely in order to launch an effective assault. An over-night pause would have given Byrhtnoth long enough to organise the men of the select fyrd whom he must have already summoned, and to call up the great fyrd of much of Essex, although the numbers of the great fyrd would depend on the speed with which its members, mostly on foot, would have been able to reach Maldon. Although the number of men that Byrhtnoth might have been able to assemble must remain a matter of conjecture, like the number of Vikings involved in the battle, it is possible to make an equally reasoned guess at numbers on the English side just as it was possible in the last chapter to calculate the probable size of the Scandinavian army. It can be deduced from Domesday Book that Essex had over 2,500 hides of land in 1086. Domesday Book is a particularly useful source of information for Essex because it is included in so-called Little Domesday, the full detail of the East Anglian return which was never included in Domesday proper as were the returns from other areas but was kept with it. If the figure of hides in Essex was similar in 991, and there is no real reason why it should have materially changed, this would suggest that, if Byrhtnoth had time to call up the whole of the select fyrd of Essex, he would have had a battle-ready army of only 500, with perhaps another 100 of his own fol-lowers, and this figure makes it easy to understand why the Viking leaders, with five times that number of experienced soldiers at their command, would consider it worth their while to engage him rather than sail away and find booty elsewhere. There is another possible reading to the Vikings' camping on Northey Island, of course. The confirmation of the will of Æthelric of Bocking, used at the end of the last chapter to suggest that it was Swein Forkbeard who commanded the Viking forces, indicates that there was a plot among at least some of the minor aristocracy in Essex to receive Swein, and if this refers to the situation in 991, not only does it explain why the Vikings made no attempt to attack the town of Maldon, but it might suggest that not all of the select fyrd responded to Byrhtnoth's call to arms. We should assume that the figure for trained men at his disposal is the maximum that Byrhtnoth might have had. The actual number may have been much smaller. In addition to his trained soldiers, Byrhtnoth undoubtedly had part of the great fyrd, however, together with able-bodied men from Maldon itself and the surrounding farms and villages which may have doubled his force, although the Domesday evidence suggests that the land south of the river was quite sparsely populated. But these auxiliaries would have been lucky to be armed with spears, and many would have had to defend themselves with the tools of their trade – woodman's axes and farmer's scythes and coulters – and were unlikely to have had any sort of shield. The great fyrd was in effect the early medieval equivalent of cannon fodder, and could be of use to their commander only so long as they were tightly controlled. The failure of the English to respond to the challenge of the Vikings at Maldon was probably due less to the military prowess of their opponents than to the loss of that control on both the national and the local level.

5

The Battle of Maldon

By their very nature, battle sites leave little in the way of archaeological remains. The English dead following the battle of Maldon would have been carried away to be given honourable burial, and the Vikings may well have dealt with their own casualties, or, if that were impossible, the English would have left them for nature to take care of, or perhaps burnt them. Material objects such as weapons and armour were useful to both sides, and

such weapons as the Vikings left on the field would have
been quickly taken by the English survivors. The Bayeux
Tapestry shows the dead being stripped of body armour.
For knowledge of most early battles we are dependent on
literary sources, and in the case of Maldon, we have a surprisingly large number. The *Anglo-Saxon Chronicle* reported
the encounter, but only (in the case of chronicle A) in the
starkest terms, noting the large size of the fleet, the outcome of the conflict and its repercussions. There is also a
short account of the battle in the *Vita Oswaldi* or Life of St
Oswald (bishop of Worcester and archbishop of York, died
988), which is a work by Byrhtferth, a monk of Ramsey,
who is known to be the author of a number of texts in the
decade or so after the fight occurred. That Byrthferth was
writing so soon after the event might be seen at first sight
as giving his work particular authority, especially as Ramsey
benefited from Ealdorman Byrhtnoth's will and might have
wished to preserve an accurate account of his death. The
abbey was a relatively minor beneficiary, however, in comparison with Ely, and the account of Byrhtnoth's fall in the
life of St Oswald has to be read in the light of its author's
habitual style, which depends more on rhetorical patterning
and grand gestures than attention to detail. After stating that
Byrhtnoth's personal retinue fought alongside him and that
he encouraged his men when they were in battle formation, he tells us that the hero of his narrative was tall and
white-haired (both confirmed by other sources), and that
he struck blows with his right hand and protected himself
with his left, unmindful of the weakness of his body. In a
particularly grandiose passage, he has him fighting in the
thick of the battle, adding, more pertinently perhaps:

> An infinite number of them and us were killed, and Byrhtnoth him-
> self was killed, and the remainder fled. The Danes too were severely
> wounded; they were scarcely able to man their ships.

For all its probable historical deficiencies, it may be deduced from this that it was generally understood at the time that the battle was a major encounter. No doubt many of the English ran away (a possibility which will be explored below), and no doubt Viking numbers were considerably depleted. But just how many of their ships were incapacitated is not clear, given the *Chronicle* report that a large sum was paid to the Vikings after the battle to prevent further depredations along the south-east coast.

Three other types of source material give us information about the battle: monastic records of Byrhtnoth's death, monastic chronicles, and the English poem now usually known as *The Battle of Maldon*. The first of these are notices deriving from the fact that Byrhtnoth, as both a pious defender of the Church party in the disputes that arose after King Edgar's death, and a generous benefactor of monasteries in his will, was remembered by the monks in their prayers on the anniversary of his death. To ensure that they commemorated him on the right day, his obit was recorded in three necrologies (lists of deceased members of the monastery or significant persons associated with it) added to calendars, originating from monasteries in Winchester, Ely and Ramsey. The Winchester obit is in a calendar written by the monk Ælsinus for Ælfwine, the deacon of the New Minster (see Plate 48). Since Ælfwine became deacon in 1023 and was promoted to abbot in 1031 or 1032, the manuscript can be dated with unusual precision. The date may be further narrowed by the entry for Ælfwine's mother, who died in 1029, which means that the calendar was written around 1030. It gives the date of Byrhtnoth's death as 11 August, and since the manuscript was written within living memory of the battle, this date may be seen as reliable. The two other obits are from less secure sources. The first records his death as 10 August and is in an Ely calendar copied at the end of the twelfth century. Though Ely is a place that particularly revered the memory of Byrhtnoth, it would not be surprising to find a slippage of one day in a calendar copied two centuries after the event. For the last calendar, made at Ramsey, we have no surviving medieval evidence but only a sixteenth-century copy of a manuscript that was lost during the dissolution of the monasteries in the 1530s, but this again records the death as occurring on 11 August, giving further confirmation of the Winchester date for the battle.

The ecclesiastical chronicles were compiled in monasteries primarily to record events that pertained to their houses, and were especially concerned to note documents and evidential matter proving how and when they acquired land, thereby proving their entitlement to their wealth. Among a number of chronicles which mention the battle and its outcome, that of John of Worcester which records the names of the Viking leaders as Justin and Guthmund was considered in Chapter 3. Of the rest of his brief account, only one sentence is significant:

> Not long afterwards Byrhtnoth, mighty ealdorman of the East Saxons, engaged in battle with them near Maldon but after an infinite multitude had been killed on both sides, the ealdorman himself fell.

The phrase 'not long afterwards' is reminiscent of the 'very soon after that' of the account of the battle of Maldon in the CDE chronicle and may well be drawn from it. If that is the case, the rest of the passage may be an imaginative elaboration of the *Chronicle* account, interwoven with material drawn from the 994 treaty that names Justin and Guthmund as present in England, together with Olaf Tryggvason. If this chronicle is not reliant on CDE, however, we have here an independent witness to the significance of the battle in terms both of the number killed on each side and of the length of the engagement – and the information supplied by John is supported by the evidence of the much earlier *Vita Oswaldi*. Although the *Vita* and John's account both

1. The Gokstad ship from Sandefjord, Vestfold, Norway, viewed from the prow. The illustration shows the relatively broad beam of the vessel.

2. The Gokstad ship viewed from the starbord side. The top of the rudder may just be seen near the stern.

3. The restored surviving parts of Skuldelev wreck 5, mounted and seen from the bow.

4. The restored surviving parts of Skuldelev wreck 5, mounted and seen from the stern.

5. Scale model of Skuldelev wreck 5 made by Morten Grønbech with rigging by Erik Andersen and Vibeke Bischoff.

6. Scale model of Skuldelev wreck 2 made by Morten Grønbech with rigging by Erik Andersen and Vibeke Bischoff.

7. *Above:* Wonderful view of the reconstruction of Skuldelev 2 under sail in Roskilde Fjord.

8. *Right:* Bow view of Skuldelev 5 in Roskilde Fjord.

9. One of the reconstructed Skuldelev vessels taking modern vikings out into Roskilde Fjord.

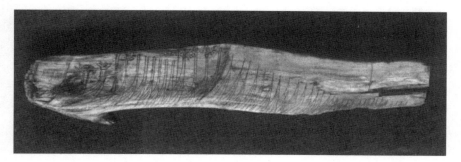

10. A thirteenth-century piece of rough timber from Bergen, Norway, 10 inches (25 centimetres) long, with an artist's impression of a fleet of 48 warships incised on one side and a runic inscription on the other, reading: 'Here the sea-bold one (= the fleet) travels'. See Figure 72.

11 and 12. A sample of a silver penny from the middle of King Edgar's reign, when different regions used different designs. By its devices (here the use of rosettes), the coin can be located in north-west Mercia. Note that there is no bust.

13 and 14. A silver penny from the end of Edgar's reign when his monetary reform had established uniformity throughout the kingdom. Now the coin has a bust in the manner of Roman coins with the emperor's head portrayed, in this case surrounded by the name *Eadgar* and his style *rex Anglorum* 'king of the English' (abbreviated). The reverse has the name of the moneyer Goldstan and the place of origin, Lewes, Sussex. This rapidly became the most sophisticated system of coinage in Europe.

15 and 16. Æthelred's first coinage, in circulation *c.* 979 – 985, has a more elaborate reverse than his father's reformed coinage, with the Hand of God flanked by the Greek letters alpha and omega. Again the moneyer and place of issue are named, here Leofstan at Canterbury.

17. Quartered and halved pennies. The two most commonly kept animals, sheep and pigs, were valued respectively at five pence and ten pence in King Æthelstan's sixth lawcode, so the penny was worth a lot of money in the period. To provide for smaller units, pennies were cut into halfpennies and farthings (Old English *feorthing* 'a fourth'), denominations that lasted until the mid-twentieth century.

18 and 19. The issue of *c.* 985 – 991, known as the 'Second Hand', shows a modified form of the previous coin on the reverse, with curled cuffs on the hand and two prominent bosses beside the fingers. In this way, it was ensured that any one quarter of the coin, when cut, would be distinguishable from the previous issue. The moneyer Oscytel, whose name may clearly be read and who produced this example, worked in London.

20 and 21. The third issue of Æthelred's reign to show the Hand of God motif followed the 'Second Hand' type *c.* 991 and displays major modification of the reverse. The hand stands alone, with two fingers extended in a 'benedictional', as seen in manuscript illuminations. This was made by the moneyer Leofric at Tamworth.

22 and 23. Although it might appear that the bust on this coin is wearing a helmet and armour, in fact the style is copied directly from late Roman coins. The issue, known as 'Helmet', was in circulation *c.* 1003 – 1009, this example having been struck by the moneyer Dreng at Lincoln.

24 and 25. The 'Agnus Dei' or Lamb of God coin, in circulation in the first decade of the new millennium and thought to be a way of invoking God's help against the vikings. Since very few coins of this type have survived, all from minor mints, it is assumed that a decision was taken very soon after the dies were issued that it would not be used.

26 and 27. Æthelred's final issue, the 'Last Small Cross', reverted to the design of his father's reform issue, see Plate 13. This example was struck by Godric at London, *c.* 1010 – 1016.

28 and 29. This is an example of the 'Crux' coin, the first of Æthelred's issues to have the head facing left rather than right as in Plates 15, 18 and 20, and is the first in the 'Cross' series, as in Plates 23 and 27. This issue circulated *c.* 991 – 997, and this particular example was made in Maldon by the moneyer Ælfwine.

30 and 31. *Right:* An example of the 'Long Cross' issue that followed the 'crux' issue and preceded the 'Helmet' issue (see Plate 22) was in circulation in the period *c.* 997 – 1003. This example was also made at Maldon by the moneyer Toga.

32, 33, 34, 35. *Above:* Two coins issued by King Swein Forkbeard of Denmark, signing himself king of the Danes. They imitate Æthelred's Crux issue (see Plate 28), but the difference in size between them, indicative of a difference in weight, shows just how inferior to the English coinage they are.

36 and 37. *Right:* A very crude imitation of an Æthelred's Crux penny issued by Olaf Tryggvason after he became king of Norway in 995.

38. *Opposite*: Page from the A-version of the *Anglo-Saxon Chronicle* (Corpus Christi College Cambridge 173, fol. 29 verso) showing entries from 984 to 1001. The scribe originally listed annal numbers down the left margin, one per line. He later erased those in lines 7 – 10 and wrote them continuously across line 6. The entry for 993 (error for 991) now begins on line 7 and runs for four lines before continuing down the left margin. Clearly this was all an afterthought on the scribe's part. The last sentence of the marginal addition was made even later by another scribe. See plan in Figure 73.

Ān·dcccc·lxxxiiii   Her forð ferde se welþillenda bisceop aðelwold

Ān·dcccc·lxxxv   ⁊ feo halgunᵹ þæs æftran fylᵹendan bisceopᵴ ælfheaᵹᵴ

Ān·dcccc·lxxxvi   se ðe oðran naman þæᵴ ᵹecïᵹed ᵹodwine xciii· kł· noū·

Ān·dcccc·lxxxvii   ⁊ heᵹefæt þōn bisceop ftol an þapa cyþᵹia apoftola aðᵹe

Ān·dcccc·lxxxviii   Simonyᵴ ⁊ iuðæ· on pintan ceafcre·

Ān·dcccc·lxxxviiii   Ān·dcccc·xc· Ān·dcccc·xci· Ān·dcccc·xcii :⁊

Ān·dcccc·xciii   Her on ðyᵴ ᵹeare com unlaf miðþᵴ ⁊ þuno ⁊ᵹonᵃᵹonᵴcipᵘ
toſtane ⁊ ſorphergedonᵴ on ytan ⁊ forða ðanon to ſanðpic ⁊ ſpaðanon toᵹipᵴ þic
þ eall oᵹerïode ⁊ ſpatᵒ mældune ⁊ hiſ ðcñeo toᵹeanᵴ byrhtnoð ealdorman miðhiſpyrðe
⁊ hī pïðᵹeſeahtᵴ ⁊ hyſ þōn ealdorman þcñ oſrloᵹon ⁊ þælſtope ᵹepeald ahtan ⁊ him man nam·

Ān·dcccc·xciiii   Her forð ferðe siᵹepic arce biſceop· ⁊ ſenᵹ ælfpic

Ān·dcccc·xcv   pïltun reſpe biſceop toðam arce biſceop pïce·

Ān·dcccc·xcvi

Ān·dcccc·xcvii

Ān·dcccc·xcviii

Ān·dcccc·xcviiii

M·

(left margin:) ᵹoddan ᵹuð þɫ / hïne naſecanᵹ / ᵹ·ððan to biſceopᵴ / anda· ðurh ſïpuᵴ / are canᵹarebiſcpᵴ / alſceageſ þï neæſᵴ ueᵭ

M· 1· Her on ðyᵴ ᵹeare þ·yy micel unᵹrïð on angel cynñᵴ lonðe þuruh ſciphere
⁊ relᵹehrcñy hergeðon ⁊ bærnðon ſpaᵴ hy upp aſecoon on ſnneſiᵭ þ hy
coman to eþelïnga ðene ⁊ þacomþcñ toᵹeanᵴ hamtun ſcïr· ⁊ hïpð
ᵹeſuhton ⁊ ðcñ pealð eþelpearð cïnᵹᵴ· heahᵹereſa oſrleᵹen
⁊ leoſpïc æt hïttinucean ⁊ leoſpïne cïnᵹᵴ· heahᵹereſa ⁊ pulſhere
biſceopᵴ ðeᵹn ⁊ ᵹoðwine æþorðiᵹe ælſſïᵹᵴ biſceopᵴ ſunu ⁊ ealra
manna an ⁊ þuno ealrattᵹ· ⁊ þ æþpearð þara ðenïƿepa miclema
oſrleᵹenna· þealðe hïe þælſtope ᵹe pealð ahtan

39. *Left*: The C-version of the *Anglo-Saxon Chronicle* (Cotton Tiberius B.i, fol. 144 verso) showing entries for the years 991 – 993.

41 and 42: *Above:* Aerial views of the southern end of Northey Island with the causeway linking it to the mainland. The view in Plate 41 looks upstream towards the town of Maldon, and the narrowing of the river beyond Northey is clear. All channels were narrower in 991. Although the modern town is much larger than it was in 991, the original site at the water's edge may just be seen.

40. *Opposite:* A copy of the confirmation by King Æthelred of the will of Æthelric of Bocking which suggests that Æthelric was involved in a plot to receive Swein in Essex earlier than 994, a clear indication that Swein was at Maldon in 991. The document was written on a single sheet of parchment three times, with the word CYROGRAPHUM in capitals between each copy. When the copies were cut, as here, there was proof that it was genuine in the other copies. In this case, one copy went to the widow, one to the king, and the third, this one (Canterbury Cathedral Chart. Ant. Bi, Red Book no. 18), to the chief beneficiary after the widow, the monastery of Christ Church, Canterbury.

43. *Top:* Maldon town seen from the causeway. The slightly higher ground on which the town is built can be seen.

44, 45, 46. *Above, left and right, and right:* The causeway looking towards Northey Island at different stages of the tide. At mean high water, the causeway is covered to a depth of six feet (1.8 metres). Although the channel was narrower in 991, the causeway was steeper and at least as deep.

47. *Right:* The causeway at low water taken from the island towards the mainland. The mainland at this point is now largely mudflats which were more extensive in 991.

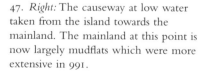

48. *Right:* Ælfwine's calendar from
Winchester (Cotton Titus D.xxvii,
fol. 6 verso) showing the entries for
August. Byrhtnoth's obit (*Obitus
Byrhtnoði comitis*) is entered at line 13.

570   *Appendix.*

Viri Vice-Comitis de Weymouth, apud palatium fuum,
vulgo voc^m. *Longleat.*

Memorand. that the said Paper was tranfcrib'd by
Mr. Robinfon, who had lately the Sinecure of Afh-
bury, and, upon his death, was fucceeded in the fame
by the forefaid Mr. George Wigan.

Num. VII. Vide §. XXV.
Bibl. Cott. Otho. A. XII. 3. Folio 57.

Fragmentum quoddam hiftoricum de Eadrico &c.
vel *Fragmentum Liftoricum, capite & calce muti-
lum, fex foliis conftans, quo Poëtice & Stylo Cæd-
moniano celebratur virtus bellica* BEORHTNO-
THI *Ealdormanni & aliorum Anglo-Saxonum,
in prælio cum Danis. Vide Smithi Catal. Bibl.
Cott. p. 67. & Hickefii Thef. l. II. p. 232.*

..... bɲocen puɲðe. het þa hýɲɽa hpæne. hoɲɽ ɲoɲ
lætan ɲeoɲ aɲýɲan ꞇ ɲoɲð ᵹanᵹan hicᵹan ꞇo hanðum
ꞇ þiᵹe ᵹoðū. þ þ oɲɽan mæᵹ æpeſꞇ on ɲunðe þ ɲe
eoɲl nolðe ýnh̃ðo ᵹeþolian he let him þa oɲ hanðon
leoɲne ɲleoᵹan haɲoc pi̊ð þæs holꞇes ꞇ ꞇo þæɲe hilðe
ſꞇop. be þa man mihꞇe oncnapan þ ſe cniht nolðe
pacian æꞇ þā p.... ᵹe þa he ꞇo pæpnū ɽenᵹ. eac hī
polðe eaðɲic hiɽ ealðɲe ᵹe læſꞇan ɲnean ꞇo ᵹeɽeohꞇe
on ᵹan þa ɲoɽð beᵹan ᵹaɲ ꞇo ᵹuþe he hæɲþe ᵹoð ᵹe-
þanc þa hpile þe he mið hanðum healðan mihꞇe boɲð
ꞇ bɲað ɽpuɽð beoꞇ he ᵹelæſꞇe þa he æꞇɽoɲan hiɽ
ɲnean ɽeohꞇan ſceolðe.

Ða þæɲ býɽhꞇno̊ð onᵹan beoɽnaɽ ꞇɽýmian. ɲað ꞇ
ɽæððe ɲincū ꞇæhꞇe hu hi ɽceolðon ſꞇanðan ꞇ þone
ſꞇeðe

49. *Left:* The page from Thomas Hearne's
*Johannis Confratis et Monachi Glastoniesis,
Chronica,* published in 1726, which shows
the opening of *The Battle of Maldon.* This
was the first printing in modern times of
the poem, and the type used is that created
by the printer John Day for the antiquarian
Matthew Parker, archbishop of Canterbury
1559–75, for his printing of religious
materials in Old English. The type was
held by Oxford University Press until the
twentieth century when it was lost.

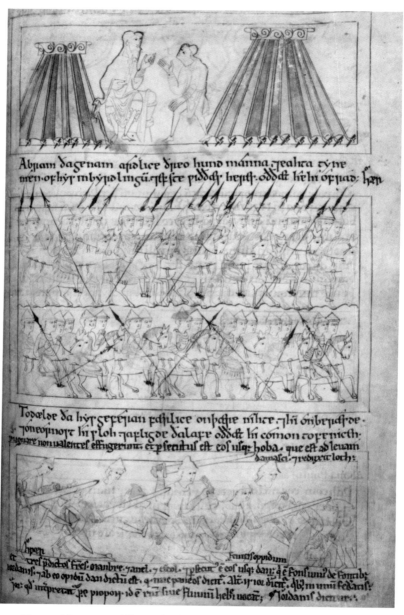

50. Mounted horsemen riding to battle, from an early eleventh-century illustrated copy of the Old English translation of Genesis (Cotton Claudius B.iv, fol. 25 recto). The bottom panel shows them fighting on foot in the battle itself.

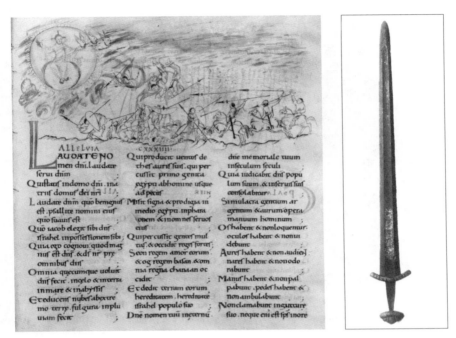

51. *Above left:* Manuscript illustration from an early eleventh century psalter (Harley 603, fol. 69 recto) showing how spears were wielded.

52. *Above right:* Sword of the ninth to tenth century from the River Thames, near Bray Mill, Buckinghamshire, typical of the period of the battle. What is now a narrow metal hilt would have been covered.

53. One of the reconstructed Skuldelev ships sailing in Roskilde Fjord. The method of hanging shields on the shield-rack along the gunwale is clearly seen, and the shields themselves are good replicas of those used by both vikings and English.

54. *Above left:* Drawing of the late medieval wall-painting of Byrhtnoth above his tomb in the north wall of the Norman quire of Ely cathedral. The drawing was made when the tomb was moved to Bishop West's chapel in the eighteenth century. From J. Bentham, *The History and Antiquities of the Conventual and Cathedral Church of Ely*, 2nd ed. (Norwich, 1812).

55. *Above right:* Bishop West chapel in Ely Cathedral, drawn before the addition of the eighteenth-century tombs of early benefactors of the abbey, together with their memorial. From J. Bentham, *The History and Antiquities of the Conventual and Cathedral Church of Ely*.

56. The memorial to the Anglo-Saxon benefactors of Ely in the Bishop West chapel.

57. *Right:* Byrhtnoth's eighteenth-century tomb, describing him as Duke of Northumbria, killed in battle by the Danes in 991.

58. *Below:* A curtained alcove, showing one use of textiles in houses of the period (Corpus Christi College Cambridge 23, fol. 38 recto). Other illustrations show them used elsewhere in living quarters and around beds.

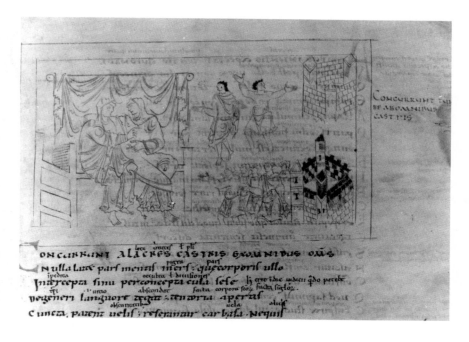

Map labels:
YORK
MERSEY
DANELAW
CHESTER • BAKEWELL
STAFFORD • DERBY
WATLING STREET
• LEICESTER
HUNTINGDON
THETFORD
BUCKINGHAM • BEDFORD
COLCHESTER
WITHAM
MALDON
THAMES
CANTERBURY
WINCHESTER

59. *Opposite*: Early Anglo-Saxon kingdoms

60. *Above*: Edward and Æthelflæd's burhs

61. Viking campaigns in England 991-1005

62. *Opposite, above*: Towns with mints in Æthelred's day

63. *Opposite, below*: Maldon and Northey Island

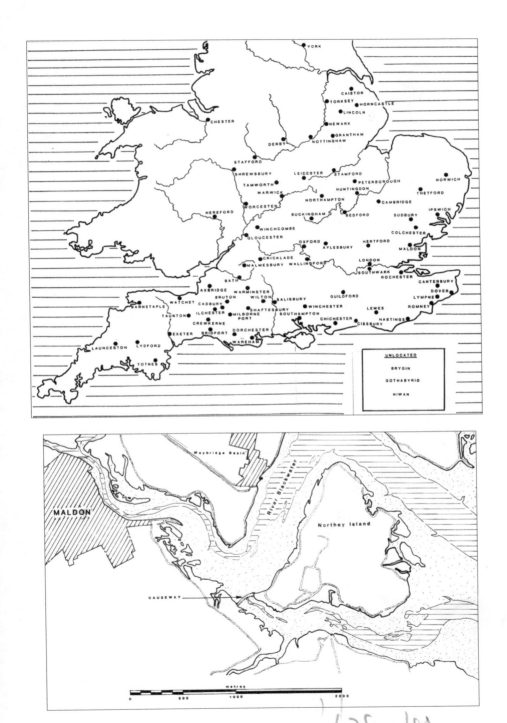

YORK

CAISTOR
TORKSEY HORNCASTLE
LINCOLN
NEWARK
CHESTER
GRANTHAM
DERBY NOTTINGHAM

STAFFORD
SHREWSBURY LEICESTER STAMFORD
TAMWORTH PETERBOROUGH NORWICH
WARWICK HUNTINGDON THETFORD
WORCESTER NORTHAMPTON
HEREFORD CAMBRIDGE IPSWICH
BUCKINGHAM BEDFORD SUDBURY
WINCHCOMBE COLCHESTER
GLOUCESTER
OXFORD AYLESBURY HERTFORD
CRICKLADE MALDON
MALMESBURY WALLINGFORD LONDON
BATH SOUTHWARK ROCHESTER
AXBRIDGE WARMINSTER CANTERBURY
BRUTON WILTON SALISBURY GUILDFORD DOVER
BARNSTAPLE WATCHET CADBURY WINCHESTER LYMPNE
TAUNTON ILCHESTER SHAFTESBURY LEWES ROMNEY
CREWKERNE MILBORNE SOUTHAMPTON HASTINGS
PORT CHICHESTER
EXETER BRIDPORT DORCHESTER CISSBURY
LAUNCESTON LYDFORD WAREHAM

TOTNES

UNLOCATED

BRYGIN

GOTHABYRIG

NIWAN

Weybridge Basin

MALDON

River Blackwater

Northey Island

CAUSEWAY

metres
0   500   1000   2000

1.25 miles

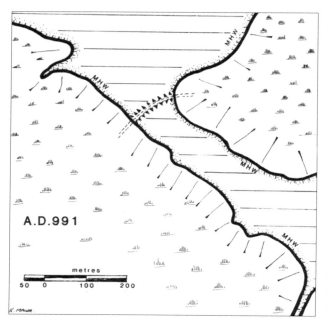

64. Estimated
coastline and
causeway in 991

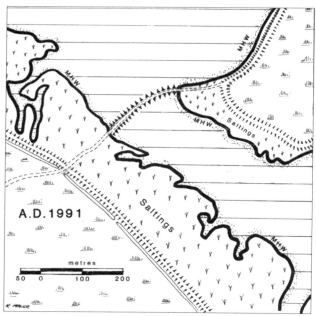

65. The causeway
in 1991

speak of the large number of dead, the actual Latin words used are different in the two versions, and therefore the reports must be considered to be independent of each other, even though, for material elsewhere in his chronicle, John is known to have drawn on the *Vita*. There are a few other later chronicles which mention the battle but all are clearly dependent on either John or the *Anglo-Saxon Chronicle*, and add nothing to the information that they afford.

There are two independent twelfth-century monastic chronicles, however, which are of significance, one at Ely and another at Ramsey. Both of these houses, as has been noted, received bequests from Byrhtnoth and from other members of his family, and they were therefore at pains to remember him and praise his generosity. As with all monastic chronicles, they were written to serve a particular agenda, notably to promote the importance and prestige of the writer's house, and they must be read with that project in mind. The *Liber Eliensis* has been mentioned in earlier chapters as a source of information on Byrhtnoth and the battle. Like all other chronicles, it borrows from earlier works, including John of Worcester's *Chronicle of chronicles* and the *Vita Oswaldi*. There are also chronological errors in much of the material presented, including the names of the abbots of both Ely and Ramsey in 991. These errors call into question the absolute reliability of statements made about the battle when the information is unconfirmed by other sources, even at points where the author is emphatic that what he says is drawn from earlier writings. Nonetheless, his testimony is patently of interest. Commenting upon Byrhtnoth's eloquence, strength and height, the writer calls him a great leader and one who fought many battles. He is eloquent in his praise of his defence of the monasteries after the death of Edgar, and continues with an account of his role in the defence of England against the Danes. It is here that we arrive at the crucial passage:

At a certain time when the Danes landed at Maldon and he heard
the news, he met them with an armed troop and destroyed nearly all
of them on a bridge over the water. Only a few of them escaped and
sailed to their own country to tell the tale. When Duke Byrhtnoth
[the Latin title is *dux*, literally Duke, presumably seen as equivalent
to *ealdorman*] returned with speed to Northumbria after this victory,
the Danes, greatly saddened with what they heard, prepared another
fleet, hurried to England, and, led by Justin and Guthmund Stectason,
landed at Maldon again after four years to avenge the killing of their
men. When they reached the harbour and heard that it was Byrhtnoth
who had done these things to their men, immediately they sent word
that they had come to avenge them, and that they would see him as
a coward if he would not undertake to join battle with them. Moved
to foolhardiness by their messengers, Byrhtnoth called together his
former companions in this affair and, led by the hope of victory and
his excessive boldness, he set out with a few warriors on the journey
to battle, taking care and hastening lest the enemy army should occupy
as much as one foot's length of land in his absence.

The features of this account that are clearly drawn from
earlier chronicles are the names of the Viking leaders and
the fact that a battle was fought by Byrhtnoth at Maldon.
It is possible that some further elements are drawn from a
copy of the Old English poem on the theme, though not
from the version that has survived to modern times, or
perhaps from a Latin summary of that work. The fact that
the fight took place on a bridge, that Byrhtnoth displayed
excessive boldness, and that he refused to allow the Vikings
one foot of land all occur in the poem, though the Old
English word *bricg* which occurs in the text of the poem that
survives means 'ford' rather than 'bridge'. The overlap is too
great to admit any other explanation than that the chronicle
is dependent to some degree on the poem. However, the
Ely chronicler's assertion that there were two battles, the
second a re-run of the first, is both unlikely and without
confirmation elsewhere. It has to be seen as error or fab-

rication, linked perhaps to the long digression that follows on the respective merits of Ramsey and Ely in terms of the fulfilment of their charitable mission. The Benedictine Rule places a clear obligation on monasteries to provide bed and board for travellers, and the Ely account records that Byrhtnoth, as he led his troops south from Northumbria, called first at Ramsey and was offered food for only himself and seven of his men – an offer to which Byrhtnoth responded in the manner of Alexander, who refused to sup before his soldier (as reported in the *Letter of Alexander to Aristotle* which was widely read in monastic circles). Ely, on the other hand, which Byrhtnoth visited next, offered 'royal hospitality', in return for which Byrhtnoth bequeathed the monastery a vast number of estates, all of which are listed, as well as a series of valuable items and quantities of gold and silver, on condition that his body was buried in the church. A number of factors point to the unreliability of this account. At over sixty years of age, Byrhtnoth would certainly have made a will disposing of his possessions long before undertaking his last battle, and would similarly have made earlier provision for his internment. More tellingly, the names of the abbots mentioned in the course of the account are incorrect. The chronicler, in short, is weaving a story of how the abbey came to be in possession of Byrhtnoth's estates to give credence to the contention that they were willed to the foundation.

The Ely account goes on to relate that the second battle of Maldon lasted for fourteen days, despite the fact that the enemy were there in greater numbers than before and Byrhtnoth had only a small number of men. It claims that on the last day, with his own army severely depleted, he almost put the Vikings to flight after considerable carnage, but they made one last push against him as a group and 'just managed to cut off his head as he fought'. Once again, that account is manifestly erroneous in some respects. No battle lasted for more than a day in this period, much less fourteen, but the claim that Byrhtnoth's head was cut off is a true one, as the chronicler would know for himself from the fact that his body, minus its head, was buried at Ely and translated to a different position within the church in the twelfth century, not long before he was in process of improving his record.

The *Ramsey Chronicle* account of the battle and of the house's relations with Byrhtnoth are, perhaps surprisingly in view of the light in which Ramsey itself is shown, remarkably similar to the Ely record. The Ramsey chronicler attempts to explain his abbot's position more fully and to belittle the generosity of Ely's abbot, but it is nonetheless apparent that the two versions are closely connected. Unlike the *Liber Eliensis*, this chronicle makes no mention of two battles at Maldon, or even one, but states that Byrhtnoth passed Ramsey by ship (technically possible since Ramsey is in the Fens) with a large number of troops and asked the abbot for food. The abbot replied that he had insufficient bread for the army as a whole but could feed Byrhtnoth and six or seven of his companions. Byrhtnoth's response again accorded with that attributed to Alexander (i.e. that it would be improper for the leader to satisfy himself while his soldiers went without) whereupon the 'shameless' abbot of Ely sent word that he would offer hospitality with 'copious provisions'. Accordingly, 'with the trivial price of their liberality' the monks of Ely gained the gratitude of Byrhtnoth and with it many of his lands, including some that had been destined for Ramsey. The chronicler nevertheless mentions two properties that Byrhtnoth did in fact grant to his house 'in a charter of King Edgar'. Although the surviving charter relating to those particular properties is a forgery, there is no doubt that Ramsey did receive them from Byrhtnoth, and that they were granted in Edgar's reign when Ramsey was founded in 966. The gifts to Ramsey are associated with Byrhtnoth's close friendship with Ramsey's founder, Ealdorman Æthelwine of East Anglia, however, rather than with any interest of his own in Ramsey itself. All other evidence suggests that Byrhtnoth's family as a whole favoured Ely, an ancient abbey which had fallen into decay under Danish rule but was re-founded by Bishop Æthelwold in 970 with King Edgar and Byrhtnoth himself as its principal lay patrons.

What factual information, then, may be deduced from the two chronicles? Ramsey's offers no information that is not in Ely, and where the two overlap, the only point of interest is that Byrhtnoth was involved with both houses. It would seem that at some point Byrhtnoth did visit both with a large entourage, but it is doubtful that this was when he was on his way to fight at Maldon. The evidence points to the Ely account being based on earlier sources, but with considerable embroidery on the part of the chronicler. One of those sources must have contained an account of the competition between the two houses for Byrhtnoth's support, but how accurate the story of the feeding of the army is can never be known. In short, neither account affords any reliable information on the marshalling and organisation of the English army in the lead-up to the battle of Maldon.

The most immediate and detailed report of the battle comes from a fragmentary vernacular poem now generally known as *The Battle of Maldon* but referred to by various titles such as *The Death of Byrhtnoth* in the nineteenth century. The work survived to the modern period in a single manuscript copy, discovered in the sixteenth century. It may have belonged to Lord Lumley in 1596 if a library catalogue entry which refers to a 'Saxon fragment' is to be identified with this text, but it certainly had come into the possession of Sir Robert Cotton (1571–1631) by 1621. Cotton was an indefatigable antiquarian who had begun to collect medieval materials when he was only seventeen years old, and the very large library that he assembled in the course of his life passed into public hands in the seventeenth century, and ultimately became an important part of the British Library. Cotton's library was unfortunately subject to a disastrous

fire in 1731, however, in which many early manuscripts per-
ished. The one which contained the poem, shelf-mark Otho
A.xii, was badly affected, and all the leaves on which the
poem was written were totally lost. Happily, before it was
burnt, the manuscript had been described and its contents
copied and published (see Plate 49), and there is no reason
to doubt its authenticity as a medieval document. Since the
manuscript itself has not survived, it is impossible to date the
copy of the poem it contained, and without the terminus
that information would have supplied, critics have vigor-
ously debated the poem's date of composition. Arguments
advanced include dates as late as the middle of the eleventh
century. In order to assign a possible time of composition to
the poem it is necessary to take careful note of the language
used, and of precisely what is said about the battle. From
a linguistic viewpoint, the best guide to the poem's date
is the form given for the name Byrhtnoth, which in the
early tenth century was spelt Beorhtnoth, and which in the
eleventh became Brihtnoth. The spelling Byrhtnoth used
throughout the poem occupies a narrow window in other
records at the end of the tenth century. If the poem was not
composed and written down at that time, its scribe had a
remarkable knowledge of late tenth-century writing habits.
As regards content, the poem offers two pieces of evidence:
first, English armour is described in terms appropriate to
conditions before 1008 but not after that date, suggesting
either the poet was composing before 1008 or that he had an
unusual understanding of military history. Secondly, the long
list of names of English participants in the battle includes
many that would be apposite to 991 but not later. Some
are names of people who had lands in Essex and might be
expected to have fought to defend them, though there is so
much repetition in the use of Anglo-Saxon names it may be
misguided to identify those named with specific individuals. Others mentioned are historical figures who are not
known to have survived beyond 991, including Byrhtnoth

himself, and Ælfwine, whom the poet calls the grandson of Ealdorman Ealhhelm of Mercia (Ealhhelm indeed having a grandson with that name). The accretion of convincing detail is so great that it seems highly unlikely that a poet writing at a distance from the battle could have achieved this degree of authenticity. It may thus be assumed that the poet was writing near enough in time to the historical event for his poem to serve as a memorial work – as the inclusion of the extensive list of names suggests. If so, it may be further assumed that the general account of the conduct of the battle given in the poem is an accurate one since the work is designed for an audience that had second- or even first-hand knowledge of the encounter. Writers close to the event, such as the compiler(s) of the *Anglo-Saxon Chronicle* and the monk Byrhtferth of Ramsey, refer to it in terms that suggest that there were many people in the England of the period who had a clear idea of what took place, and there must also have been a large local community to whom those named in the poem would have been known. The poem could function as a memorial only if it was directed towards an audience familiar with the participants, able to appreciate the extolling of their deeds, and acquainted, from survivors, with the general conduct of the battle.

Before considering how far the information supplied by the poem is reliable, however, it is necessary to recall the nature of poetry itself. While it is true that history in the form of a chronicle may be written in verse, if the composition displays other poetic devices, for example the use of imagery, it becomes extremely difficult to distinguish the factual elements of the poem from the imaginative arena that the writer creates. In the case of *The Battle of Maldon*, the poet's imaginative engagement with his narrative is clear in aspects of his work. He assigns speeches to his characters, for example, and describes their thoughts and intentions, neither of which can directly reflect events in the heat of battle. *The Battle of Maldon* may be seen, in fact, not as

versified history but as a type of epyllion, a literary form
which describes a single heroic incident from the past, epic
in theme and tone but shorter than the conventional epic,
and narrower in scope. Of course, the length of the original
poem can only be guessed at, but the narrative structure as it
has come down to us points to relatively little having been
lost. Although both the beginning and end are missing, there
is good reason to assume that what is lacking is a general
introduction to the battle, and a heroic conclusion in which
the remainder of the vanquished die heroically. Descriptions
of the manuscript before it was burnt make clear that the
poem survived on three parchment sheets folded to make
six folios or twelve pages, and they were perhaps preserved
as part of the binding of a later medieval book. Since in the
Anglo-Saxon period manuscripts regularly consisted of four
sheets folded to make an eight-leaf quire, it is a reasonable
speculation that no more than a single outer leaf has been
lost. This means, to judge by the surviving material, that
about fifty lines of verse have been lost at the beginning
and the same number at the end, or rather less if the poem
ended before the bottom of the last page.

That the material has been shaped according to a literary convention is evident from the characterisation of the
English participants. The most enduring image in all surviving Old English verse is that of a chieftain surrounded
by a band of his close companions. The leader binds his
followers to him by rich gifts which he offers at a ceremony
during a feast in his hall, and they, in turn, vow absolute
loyalty to him. This image was extended by Christian writers to stories from both the Old and the New Testaments.
Abraham is a war-lord with his warrior band in the Old
English *Genesis*, and in what is regarded as the earliest use
of the inherited heroic form for Christian use, the Hymn
to the Creation by the cow-herd Caedmon, God builds
the earth as a hall for men and fills it full of treasures for
them, and it is implied, though not stated, that they then

owe him absolute loyalty. Christ too is seen as a leader, the term generally used in Old English for him being *Drihten* which is precisely the word used in other contexts for the leader of a troop of men (*driht*).

It is in this guise of a Germanic warrior lord with his loyal followers beside him that Byrhtnoth is portrayed by the *Maldon* poet (cf. Byrhtnoth identified as a giver of treasure in lines 278 and 290), and it is through this image that the poet turns his poem into an essay on loyalty, with those men who die beside their leader and thus fulfil their vows being victorious even in defeat. Unusually, however, where traditional poetry of this genre in Old English is concerned only with aristocratic life and the warfare that accompanied it, the poet of *Maldon* takes care to include all social classes in the pact of loyalty represented by the poem, even the peasant Dunnere (lines 255–6), and it is here that fiction may well blur with fact. There is no doubt that all social classes did take part in this battle, but it is also true that the ancestral heroic code applied much less to them than the legal obligation to fight for the king or his representative in defence of the country. In using the poem as evidence, it is therefore necessary to distinguish between the poet's purpose, to glorify the dead, and those details of his narrative which reflect aspects of what actually happened on 11 August 991. One such act of transference between historicity and conformity to a poetic tradition occurs with the flight of some of the English troops. The poet condemns those who run away from the battle after Byrhtnoth's death, not for desertion (i.e. a contemporary legal obligation), but for disloyalty. The characters are led by Godric son of Odda, who is portrayed as a member of Byrhtnoth's personal entourage, who has received, amongst other gifts, 'many a horse' (line 188), yet he steals Byrhtnoth's own horse to escape, the ultimate abrogation of the heroic code. Many critics have noted that, in contrast to the *Anglo-Saxon Chronicle*, the poem makes no mention of the names of the Vikings who took part in the attack, and it has been suggested that this may be a product of ignorance or the mutilation of the text. In terms of the structure of the poem, however, it is clear that the Vikings are no more than a mechanism, the cause of the battle, and the real juxtaposition is not between the opposing forces but between the men who are loyal to their lord and those who are not. The point is that at every turn this witness to the event has to be seen as a work of art and not as a factual account, and must therefore be subject in this context to a species of decoding.

According to the poem, Byrhtnoth's army consisted of two groups, a trained force of professional troops surrounding the leader himself, presumably the select fyrd but modified here to represent Byrhtnoth's personal followers as in the older heroic tradition, together with a larger body of less well-trained and less well-armed levies, i.e. the great fyrd. It would appear that the army was gathered at some distance from the battlefield, perhaps within the town of Maldon, where tactics were discussed and, no doubt, a rallying call was made, since late in the poem (lines 198–201) the character Offa is made to speak of a meeting 'earlier in the day', before the battle, where 'many spoke bravely'. The reference occurs at the point when many of the English flee, and since it is confirmed in other sources that there was indeed a flight – inevitable once the leader was known to have died – the flight may be accepted as an accurate reflection of what took place. The mention of the meeting at this juncture adds little to the poet's construction of the event, other than to confirm perhaps Offa's view that the loyalty of many was suspect from the start, and thus there is no reason to doubt that the meeting actually occurred. After this meeting the troops would then have travelled to the battlefield, many of them on horseback, an inference confirmed by the fact that the fragment opens with Byrhtnoth ordering that the horses be driven away. Not all of the members of the English army would have had horses, and it may seem that the use of horses by the citizens of Maldon – or indeed anyone travelling the short distance to the battlesite from the town – would hardly have been necessary, especially as English armies at the time fought on foot without the use of cavalry (Plate 50). Even at Hastings, seventy years later, Harold and his household were not mounted during the battle if the evidence of the Bayeux Tapestry may be relied on. But the horse was a sign of rank and wealth during this period, and it is likely that the select fyrd would all have used their horses as a matter of course. But the whole issue of the use of horses at Maldon is complicated by the way in which the poet uses the horse motif in the poem. First, the driving away of the horses is linked to courage in two ways. At the start of the fragment, Byrhtnoth exhorts the men to think about the performance of brave deeds as they advance on foot, and the poet cites a young, inexperienced warrior recognising that his leader would not tolerate cowardice. The driving off of the horses thus signals that there would be no ignominious flight if the encounter proved hard. This is clearly an imaginative reconstruction of an event, rather than unmediated fact. At the same time, however, Byrhtnoth apparently retains his horse in that he rides up and down his battle line to ensure that the troops are in the right position. Though not overtly stated, this indicates to the listening or reading audience that every member of the English side knew that Byrhtnoth's horse was still on the field of battle, and thus prepares for the turning point of the conflict. When Byrhtnoth is killed, one of his immediate entourage betrays him by escaping on his leader's horse, and the army as a whole naturally assumes that the rider is Byrhtnoth himself. This is the reason that the poet gives, through one of his characters, for the breaking of the English battle line and the fleeing of so many of the English troops. Clearly the use of the horse motif here is part of the structural design and cannot be relied upon as hard fact. The most that can be said is that some of the army arrived on horseback, but that the engagement was fought on foot.

The theme of fidelity is established at the beginning of the fragment with two cameos of individuals who show enduring loyalty to their lord, an aristocratic youth who is identified only as a relative of a senior member of Byrhtnoth's household and who rides to the battle with a hawk on his wrist (not, as some have suggested, because he was not taking the situation seriously but as a badge of his rank), and a named warrior, Eadric. The young noble-man causes his hawk to fly off to the wood, a sign that he has no expectation that he will survive the battle. Hawks take a great deal of time and patience to train, and are very personal to the owner since they can only be taught to return to the wrist of their trainer. For the youth to release his hawk indicates his acceptance that he would never go hawking again, and the poet makes the point as an indica-tion of his resolve. Similarly, Eadric steps forward boldly with his weapons, intending to use them 'as long as' he could. In each case, the image is doom–laden, implying that neither would return home safely. These are the first, in the poem as it survives, of a long list of brief portraits of brave individuals amongst the English who maintain fortitude in the face of the enemy. Although an Eadric almost certainly died in the battle, and his name appears here as part of the poet's purpose to provide a memorial roll-call, the thoughts and intentions assigned to him are clearly fictitious.

The next section of the poem is entirely credible. It has Byrhtnoth lining his troops up along the bank of a river named later in the poem as the Pant, an early name for the Blackwater, the headwaters of which are called the Pant to this day. He told them 'how they should form up and hold their position' (line 19), and that they should grasp their shields properly. The shield-wall formation, a line of interlocking shields which the enemy was forced to charge against, was crucial to Anglo-Saxon battle tactics, as both literary and iconographic depictions make clear. In this instance, with a large number of untrained troops facing an experienced foe, the army could only hope to stand firm by keeping the Vikings from getting into their ranks and thus able to attack them from both front and rear. Whether or not Byrhtnoth did actually ride up and down his lines personally, as the poet maintains, he would certainly have needed someone to do so, to ensure that the shield-wall was solid and correctly formed. The poet's use of the riding motif has already been discussed, but Byrhtnoth (or his substitute) would certainly have used his horse for this purpose both for speed and the height that it gave him. Following the inspection of the shield-wall, the poet describes the ealdor-man dismounting among his most trusted companions, contributing to the traditional heroic leader/loyal follower image which runs through the poem, and continuing the theme of loyalty which is so important to the poet's message. There may also be dramatic irony here in that it is one of those trusted followers who is close to where Byrhtnoth ultimately falls who uses his horse to escape and who is thus responsible for the loss of the battle. Obviously, none of this portion of the poem is verifiable and must be seen in terms of an imaginative reconstruction of the event.

The poem continues with an exchange, in direct speech, between Byrhtnoth and a messenger from the Vikings, in which the latter demands tribute in return for peace and the former scornfully rejects the offer, commenting deri-sively that it would be shameful for the Vikings to leave without a fight having travelled such a long way. What is taking place here is the characterisation of the two sides. Byrhtnoth is presented as brave, loyal to his king, and capa-ble of speaking without hesitation on behalf of the army, of whose loyalty he is confident. The Viking's speech is larded with expressions that a contemporary audience would have recognised as Norse influenced, while Byrhtnoth uses legal terminology (e.g. 'arbitrate', line 60) appropriate to a man who regularly presided at the shire court. Though providing a convincing representation of reality, two things militate against the exchange as a factual account. In the first place, there is no recorded precedent for the payment of tribute in the later tenth century before the battle took place, and while that does not in itself prove that the Vikings might not have asked for payment, it does cast doubt on a piece of evidence which may be no more than an anachronistic device on the part of the poet designed to elevate the central figure. Knowing that tribute was subsequently paid, a contemporary audience would be unlikely to question the precise sequence of events. The second difficulty with the passage is a practical one. It is not easy to envisage an exchange of complex messages across a river which was sufficiently broad, as demonstrated by subsequent events, to prohibit the participants from crossing or using any weapon effectively except for a bow. A 'fliting' or scolding dispute was a regular feature of heroic verse before the onset of a physical encounter, and this exchange should probably be seen as part of this tradition.

Byrhtnoth, according to the poet, then ordered his men to advance their formation until they were lined up along the bank, presumably so that the Vikings would have to attack them by climbing out of the river and the mud that lay beneath the water. At this point the poet becomes much more specific about topography in that he makes it clear that the Vikings were at the opposite side of a channel from the English, across which there was a causeway, covered at the start of the encounter by the tide. There has been much speculation on the relevance of these details to the site of the battle, ranging from an assumption that the poet knew the area and made intelligent guesses about the conduct of the action without any specific facts on which to draw, to the assertion that he had detailed knowledge of the battle and was accurately identifying Northey Island as the Viking camp and its causeway as the place of the encounter. It was suggested above that linguistic features of the poem and details of the weaponry used indicate that it was composed close in time to the battle, and the nature of the composition as a memorial indicates that it was intended for an audience which would know something of the fight itself. It is inherently unlikely in these circumstances that the causeway – described in terms which correlate with that to Northey Island – is the poet's invention. A detailed geological survey has shown that the channel south of the island in 991 was much narrower than it is today, little more than 120 yards (100 metres) at high tide, with a depth of water across the causeway of almost six feet (two metres). This would be too deep for a man to venture across against an armed enemy and would explain the pause that occurs in the poem before the two sides are able to meet. The fact that a pause is said to have occurred, however, is not in itself hard evidence of the geographical situation, as a pregnant pause before a battle is an effective and well-used literary device. But an experienced and able commander such as Byrhtnoth would obviously have advanced his men to the river at full tide, knowing that the Vikings would be unable to reach them until his battle-line was prepared. When in the poem the Vikings cross the causeway during the ebb-tide, they are said to travel west (line 97), and the existing causeway does indeed cross to the mainland in a south-westerly direction, the simplifying of the compass point being arguably dictated by the poet's metre. Nevertheless Northey is not the only possible site for a battle which could reasonably be described, as in all contemporary accounts, as taking place 'at Maldon'. Downstream of Northey is a larger island, Osea, and this too has a causeway connecting it to the mainland. In this case, however, the causeway ends at the north bank of the river, whereas Maldon, like Northey, is on the south bank. If the Vikings intended to attack Maldon and beached their ships at Osea, they would have had to cross the river again to do so. Closer again to the mouth of the Blackwater is a third island, Pewit, but this now has no causeway and is probably too far from Maldon to be described by the carto-graphically sensitive Anglo-Saxons as being near that town. Other islands off the north bank of the river are as close to Colchester as to Maldon, and a battle taking place there would hardly have been recorded as 'at Maldon'. Generally, the accumulation of evidence thus suggests that the Vikings were camped on Northey Island, and the identification is as safe as is possible at this distance in time.

The geological survey of the area around Northey has concluded that the bank of the channel dividing Northey from the south shore of the river was firmer than it is today, and relatively steep, giving the English troops a slight advantage as they stood against the Viking attack. The poet indicates that bows were used to send flights of arrows across the flooded channel, but gives no exact details of casual-ties inflicted in this way. This omission may derive from the fact that he is at pains to stress that when the battle proper begins, the first man to die on the English side at least (and the death of Englishmen is his only concern) is a relative of Byrhtnoth (lines 113–5), his sister's son to be precise, chosen no doubt because in heroic society there is a special relationship between a man and his sister's son to whom the former has an obligation of protection. The death of his kinsman is a device to heighten Byrhtnoth's close personal involvement in the battle and should not be seen as historically accurate. The man may well have died in the battle but was extremely unlikely, given the arrow shower, to have been the first of the English to do so. As the tide receded, the poem records that the commander chose three named warriors to protect the ford. Three men would undoubtedly be sufficient to protect a causeway six feet (two metres) wide, still partly covered by the tide and with deep water on either side. The deployment of a vanguard to cut down as many Vikings as possible before the main attack would be an obvious military tactic in this situation, although the position was not one that a warrior could maintain for long, as the poem indicates in the ominous phrase 'as long as they could wield weapons' (line 83). Of the three men named by the poet, it has been suggested that the first, Wulfstan, may have been the owner of the manor closest to the causeway, since a son of a man called Wulfstan disposed of an estate in the area in his will, dated seven years after the battle. The name Wulfstan, however, is a common one, and the evidence is therefore inconclusive. Another of the three names, Maccus, is an anglicised form of Norse Magnus, and this man may have been put into the front line because of his Scandinavian connections or even his previous life as a Viking. But again there is no supporting record to strengthen speculation of this kind.

With the Vikings still confined to the island, the poet introduces a further exchange between the two sides in which the Vikings, using 'guile' (line 86), ask for leave to cross the causeway and thus by implication to fight on more equal terms. Byrhtnoth, 'because of his pride' (line 89), agrees and allows the Vikings 'too much land' (line 90). Much critical ink has been spilt on this crux, some suggesting that the poet is accurately recording that Byrhtnoth's overweening self-esteem was the cause of the English defeat, others maintaining that any responsible English general would have wished to engage the Vikings while he had an army in place rather than allowing them to sail away and attack a less well-defended site. Whatever the force of the poet's comment, the terrain on which the encounter took place suggests that the huge weight of Viking numbers, with battle adrenalin rushing through their blood, must quickly have overwhelmed any attempt to defend the causeway, whatever the resistance. Indeed, the poet makes clear why he thinks the battle was lost at a later stage in his account (see below). In short, neither the motivation of the commander nor some presumed tactical advantage would have had much to do with the Vikings crossing the ford. The poet's introduction of the second exchange relates once again to his characterisation of the hero, in that he places the outcome in God's hands. His piety was clearly of great moment to the poet (he dies, for example, with a prayer for his soul), and this is consistent with the preservation of the poem in a monastic environment and perhaps with its composition there too. It must be remembered, however, that many men survived the battle and the notion that the English forces pulled back to allow the Vikings to cross the ford may therefore have some basis in fact. Rather than having three men only guarding the ford, Byrhtnoth may have placed an elite group (perhaps headed by the three named men) at the end of the crossing to take out as many of the Vikings as possible before any of them could reach firm ground. The attack would surely have begun before all of the water had ebbed from the causeway, and, with very deep water on either side, whatever their weight of numbers they would have suffered heavy casualties without making any significant headway. In these circumstances, they might well have withdrawn to the island end of the crossing, and the English general may have seen the likelihood that, if they elected to return to their ships, he would have lost the opportunity for a major confrontation while he had significant numbers at his command. Thus a tactical pulling back from the ford may have been effective, to entice the Vikings across.

The poet gives few details of either tactics or strategy during the battle itself. The account is largely taken up with single combat encounters which include some information about fighting methods, largely couched in traditional poetic phraseology, and therefore difficult to correlate with the historic event. There is little likelihood that the precise manner in which individuals died would have been known after the encounter, even the death of Byrhtnoth himself. All Old English poetic battles refer to the 'beasts of battle' (line 106), the wolf, the raven and the eagle, that traditionally feast on corpses when the warriors have finished their work. Here the wolves are the Vikings (line 96), appropriately, from the poet's point of view, in that it incorporates them into a de-personalising motif. Some reliance can be placed, however, on the emphasis on spears as the weapon of choice (lines 67, 77, 124, 138–40, 226, 230, 237, 255, 262, 310 and 321–2) for the English warriors, although Vikings use them too (lines 134, 149 and 253). There is no reference to English body-armour or helmets, only shields linked to form a defensive wall, and this tactic is mentioned on more than one occasion (lines 102, 277 and 242). Spears are frequently described as being used for throwing (by the English at lines 108–9, 150 and 321–2, and by a Viking at line 134) but sometimes it is suggested that they were also used for thrusting (lines 138 and 226). The poet indicates, moreover, that the men carried more than one weapon of this kind (line 143). If they fought with spears in their right hands and those with swords kept them in their belts until their spears were lost, the shield in the left hand was of major importance for both defence and offence. Archaeological and iconographic evidence shows that the shield was round and made of wood covered with leather, and that it had a heavy metal boss at the centre, guarding the hand that held it, as well as a metal rim. Use of the shield as more than a simple defensive weapon is indicated in the poem. The poet describes how, when wounded, Byrhtnoth used the edge of his shield to snap the shaft of the spear that had pierced him, and caused the end to vibrate until it was dislodged (lines 136–7). An enemy might also be given a blow with the shield at close quarters. In engaging an opponent with the sword, it was important, according to the poet, to first break the metal rim of his shield, as the wooden planks which it held together would then disintegrate (lines 283–4). Bows and arrows are also mentioned in the poem a number of times (lines 71, 110 and 269), and a few of the English are described as using swords (lines 15, 117–8, 162–3, and 324), as are the Vikings (lines 114 and 253). There is no mention of the battleaxe in the course of the poem, but since this weapon never occurs in Anglo-Saxon heroic verse, little can be deduced from this fact other than that the poet is conforming to a literary tradition. Interestingly, only the Vikings are said to have body-armour (line 284), but it is not clear from the poem as it survives whether the writer understood the Vikings to have deployed a shield-wall. The single significant reference (line 277) is ambiguous since it is not clear whether Edward the Tall breached theirs or his own in order to reach the enemy.

Iconographic evidence adds a little to our knowledge of how the two sides would have fought. Illustrations in manuscripts show long spears one and a half times the length of the men holding them, making them around eight feet (two and half metres) long. They are held in the right hand high above the head and the users seem to thrust downwards (Plate 51), perhaps to get inside an opponent's body-armour or behind his shield. Beyond this, most of our information about the conflict has to be deduced from the poem. The throwing spears were probably not thrown at random in the way that arrows were loosed, but directed at a specific target. The description in the poem of Byrhtnoth's own, ultimately fatal, encounter with the Vikings indicates that he aimed his first spear at the neck of his opponent where the body-armour and the helmet left a gap, and, when the enemy was disabled (and presumably with the shield-guard dropped), threw a second spear through the corselet. Whereas the deadly part of the spear was its point, that of a sword was its edge, allowing the weapon to be used in a slashing motion to disable limbs. The poet reports that Byrhtnoth's arm was cut through (lines 164–5) when he tried to draw his own sword, indicating that the spear was used first in hand-to-hand encounters. Though the importance of the shield-wall is emphasised, no information is supplied on the way that it was formed, but the Bayeux Tapestry may be helpful here in that it shows a line of men with overlapping shields. By 1066, however, warriors were encased in body-armour, and their shields are generally portrayed as kite-shaped, a style designed for fighting on horseback where the tapering end of the shield protected the rider's left leg. At Maldon, warriors must have thrust their spears at the advancing Vikings while using the barrier of shields to protect one another against any of the enemy who penetrated beyond the line of deadly points. It has to be assumed that there would have been a body of men behind the front lines to fill any breach that occurred, and that the line extended along the bank of the Blackwater in a curve to end in each direction at the river in order to prevent any Vikings from outflanking the English troops.

Byrhtnoth, according to the poet, was appropriately well accoutred. As a wealthy aristocrat and lord of the land he was defending, he was suitably attired in an ornamented robe (line 161), with torques on his arms made of gold (lines 160–1). His horse too was fit for a prince, the saddle symbolising the throne that he would occupy when at home in his hall. When the traitor Godric rode away on Byrhtnoth's horse (line 190), causing the rout that followed the lord's death, one of the crimes severely castigated by the poet is that he sat on his lord's 'trappings', i.e. his saddle. At Byrhtnoth's death, the Vikings tried, according to the poet, to steal his valuable possessions. Two words for (gold) rings are used in the description of his accoutrements (*beagas* and *hringas*, lines 160–1), and his golden-hilted sword is mentioned at line 166. The word for gold in this last instance, *fealo*, is particularly carefully chosen as it is one of many words for yellow in Old English and corresponds to the modern word 'fallow'. It carries the same overtones of brownish yellow that it has today, and denotes a colour reminiscent of falling leaves. The reference comes at the point when Byrhtnoth's sword falls to the ground because his arm has been disabled, both literally and metaphorically. The finery attributed to

Byrhtnoth is appropriate to a high-ranking aristocrat, and must correspond on some level with actuality. Similarly he is described as being flanked by two close companions, one of them a boy, who would certainly have been present in such a conflict to hold his standard and, presumably, his horse. According to the poet, both attendants died with him, and since they are named, their presence at the battle may be taken as fact. Some space is given in the poem to the boy who, it is implied, was unused to warfare, but the heroic poignancy of his death detracts from its evidential value. He is described as avenging Byrhtnoth's death by pulling out the spear that had wounded his lord and throwing it back with such dexterity that Byrhtnoth's killer was brought down. Were this true, it would imply that the boy was himself unarmed.

As far as strategy is concerned, the only significant point to be deduced from the poem is that the English shield-wall was crucial to the outcome of the conflict. Once Godric flees on Byrhtnoth's horse and is seen by many of the rank and file who assume him to be their commander, they too turn and flee and the day is lost. The poet puts this information into the mouth of Offa (lines 237–43) who appears to be the most experienced English soldier after Byrhtnoth and may well have been his second-in-command. The length of the battle cannot be determined from the poem. The reference to an assembly (lines 198–9) might be to a conference that took place earlier on the day of the battle or possibly on the day prior to the encounter. Unless victory was assured, the Vikings would probably not have risked being cut off from their boats by an incoming tide, so it may be presumed that Byrhtnoth was killed before the tide turned on 11 August. On that day (a Tuesday), there was low water at sunrise (04.43 hours), but given the fact that there was no moon (there was a new moon on 12 August) and if the poet is accurate in his assertion that the battle took place after a standoff, it is unlikely that the conflict began at this time, i.e. during the hours of darkness. The second low tide was at 17.20, which suggests that the battle may not have begun before late afternoon, and since sunset was at 19.19, there would have been little time for an extended fight, even allowing for a lengthy twilight. Brief as the encounter may have been, however, it is clear that many of the English besides Byrhtnoth himself died, and this could not have been the case without equally significant losses on the Viking side. Both the *Vita Oswaldi* and the poem suggest that both armies suffered heavy casualties, and this may be taken as fact. The battle of Maldon was a major engagement, and had Byrhtnoth lived to ensure that the English fought on, its outcome might have been very different. Given what followed, his death may be seen as one of the major turning points of English history.

APPENDIX

THE BATTLE OF MALDON

The poem on the battle is one of the liveliest and most exciting pieces of narrative verse in Old English, as well as being our fullest and most valuable source of information on the battle. It is therefore presented here in a literal, line-by-line translation, with Anglo-Saxon names that do not survive being retained in their Old English forms, and with no attempt being made to make the syntax and word-order of the original poem conform to normal prose syntax and word-order of the present day. In particular, the iterative style which is normal for poetry of the period, with words and phrases being repeated from one line to the next, is reproduced here, and the word-imagery, which includes many compounds, is translated literally so that the reader

can get something of the flavour of the original. Heroic
devices, such as the Vikings asking for tribute in the form
of gold rings, the lord's reward to his faithful followers,
are also retained. The term ealdorman, the legal term for
Byrhtnoth's office, is replaced in the poem by *eorl*, literally
'an aristocratic warrior', which fits the heroic mode, and
this is translated by its modern equivalent 'earl'. Finally, it
has become conventional in the modern printing of Old
English verse that the first letter of each line is not capital-
ised, as it is post-medieval verse, and this practice is retained
here.

> ... was broken.
> Then [Byrhtnoth] commanded each of the warriors to abandon his
> horse,
> to drive it away and to advance on foot,
> to concentrate on brave deeds and bold thoughts.
> When the kinsman of Offa first realized   5
> that the earl would not tolerate cowardice,
> he caused the much loved creature to fly from his wrist,
> his hawk off to the wood, and he himself advanced to the battle;
> by his action all would know that the youth did not intend
> to weaken in the fight when he grasped his weapons.   10
> Similarly Eadric intended to support his lord,
> his leader in the battle; he set off then to carry
> his spear to the fray; he maintained great courage
> as long as he was able to wield with his hands
> his shield and broad sword; he fulfilled his vow   15
> when he had need to fight close by his lord.
>   Then Byhtnoth set about drawing up the men there,
> he rode and instructed, he told the soldiers
> how they should form up and hold the position,
> and he asked that they should hold their shields properly,   20
> firmly with their fists, and not be at all afraid.
> When he had arrayed his troops appropriately,
> he dismounted amongst the people where it most pleased him to be,

where he knew his household companions to be most loyal.

  Then appeared on the opposite bank, called out fiercely, 25
a messenger of the vikings, he made a speech,
a man who threateningly relayed from the vikings
a message to the earl where he stood on the river bank:
'Bold seafarers have sent me to you,
commanded me to tell you that you must quickly send 30
gold rings in return for protection. And it is better for you all
that you should buy off this onslaught of spears with tribute-money
than that we should join battle very grievously.
We need not destroy each other if you are sufficiently wealthy:
we are prepared to establish a truce in return for the gold. 35
If you, the person who is in charge here, accept this,
that you are willing to ransom your people,
willing to give to the seafarers, in an amount determined by them,
money in exchange for peace, and to accept protection from us,
we are content to embark with the taxes, 40
to set sail across the sea, and to keep the peace with you all.'

  Byrhtnoth made a speech, he raised his shield,
waved his slender spear, spoke out with words,
the angry and resolute one gave him an answer:
'Sea raider, can you hear what this army is saying? 45
They intend to give all of you spears as tribute,
deadly points and tried swords,
payment in a tax of war-gear which will be of no benefit to you in
battle.
Messenger of the seamen, report back again!
Tell your people a much less pleasing tale, 50
that here stands with his company an earl of unstained reputation
who intends to defend this homeland,
the kingdom of Æthelred, that of my lord,
the people and the country. They shall fall,
the heathens in battle. It appears to me too shameful 55
that you should return to your ships with our money
unopposed, now that you thus far in this direction
have penetrated into our territory.

You will not gain treasure so easily:
spear and sword must first arbitrate between us,   60
the grim game of war, before we pay tribute.'
    Then he ordered them to pick up their shields, the warriors to
march forward,
until they all stood on the bank of the river.
Because of the water there, neither group could reach the other:
there the floodtide had come after the ebb,   65
the tidal streams had locked up the land. It seemed to them too long
to the time when they could wield spears against one another.
They stood there in military array on either side of the River
Blackwater,
the vanguard of the East Saxons and the raiders from the boats;
not one of them could harm another   70
except where someone was felled by the flight of an arrow.
The tide went out. The sailors stood ready,
many vikings, eager for battle.
Then the protector of warriors [= Byrhtnoth] commanded to hold
the causeway
an experienced soldier called Wulfstan,   75
as bold in war as were many of his family – he was Ceola's son;
he cut down with his spear the first man
who stepped with great daring onto the causeway there.
With Wulfstan stood there the fearless warriors
Ælfhere and Maccus, a brave pair   80
who refused to take flight from the ford;
rather they defended themselves staunchly against the enemy
for as long as they could wield weapons.
    When they recognized and clearly saw
that they had come up against unrelenting guardians of the causeway
there,   85
then the hateful visitors started to use guile:
they asked to be allowed to have passage,
to cross over the ford, to advance their troops.
Then because of his pride the earl set about
allowing the hateful race too much land;   90

over the chill water then began to call
the son of Byrhthelm [= Byrhtnoth] (warriors listened):
'Now a path is opened for you: come quickly against us,
men at war. God alone knows
who will control the battlefield.'   95
    Then the wolves of slaughter rushed forward, they cared nothing
for the water,
the host of vikings, west across the Blackwater,
across the shining stream they carried their shields,
the sailors carried their lime-wood shields onto the land.
There against the fierce ones stood ready   100
Byrhtnoth with his men. He commanded that with the shields
they form the battle-hedge [= shield-wall], and that the company
hold out
firm against the fiends. Then the fight was near,
glory in battle: the time had come
when those fated to die must fall there.   105
The roar of battle was lifted up there; ravens circled,
the eagle eager for carrion; there was bedlam in the land.
They released the file-hard spears from their hands then,
made fly the fiercely sharpened ones, the darts.
Bows were busy, shield absorbed spearhead.   110
The onslaught of battle was terrible; warriors fell
on either side, young men lay dead.
Wulfmær was wounded, he chose a bed of death,
Byrhtnoth's kinsman: he was with swords,
his sister's son, cruelly cut to pieces.   115
Recompense was paid to the vikings there:
I heard tell that Edward slew one
mightily with his sword, he did not withhold the blow,
so that the doomed warrior fell at his feet.
His lord gave thanks to him for that,   120
to the chamberlain, when he had opportunity.
So the valiant ones supported one another,
the warriors in the battle, directed their minds eagerly
to which of them might first with his spear there

wrest life from a doomed man,   125
soldiers with weapons. The dead fell to the ground.
        The steadfast ones held out, Byrhtnoth encouraged them,
urged that each warrior should keep his mind on the battle
who hoped to win glory from the Danes.
Then one who was hardened in war came forward, lifted up his
weapon,   130
his shield for defence, and moved against the last-named man.
Equally resolute, the earl turned towards the peasant:
each of them intended harm to the other.
Then the warrior from the sea despatched a spear of southern manu-
facture
in such a way that the lord of warriors was wounded.   135
Then [Byrhtnoth] thrust violently with the shield so that the spear-
shaft fragmented,
and the spearhead vibrated until it was dislodged.
The man of battle was incensed: with a javelin he stabbed
the proud viking who had given him the wound.
The military man was experienced: he made his spear pass   140
through the younger man's neck; his hand guided it
so that he wrenched life from the wicked thief.
Then he quickly despatched another,
so that the body-armour shattered: he was wounded in the breast,
through the ringmail; at his heart stood   145
the deadly point. The earl was the more exultant:
the proud man roared with laughter, gave thanks to his Maker
for the day's work that the Lord had given him.
Then one of the Danes caused to fly a dart from his hand,
made it travel through the air from his fist, so that it went too
far   150
through the noble one, the thegn of Æthelred.
By his side stood a young man not yet fully grown,
a squire in the battle, who very bravely
pulled the bloody spear from the warrior,
Wulfstan's son, Wulfmær the Younger;   155
he hurled that hardest of objects back again;

the point went in so that the very one was laid low
who had severely wounded his lord just then.
 Then an armed man approached the earl;
he wanted to acquire that warrior's armrings,   160
the robe and gold bands, and the ornamented sword.
Then Byrhtnoth drew the sword from its sheath,
broad and with a shining blade, and struck at the corselet.
Too quickly one of the seamen prevented him,
when he disabled the earl's arm.   165
The the golden-hilted sword fell to the ground:
he could not hold the formidable blade,
wield his weapon. Still then he might make a speech,
the grey-haired warrior, encourage the younger men,
bid his brave companions press forward.   170
He could not then stand firmly on his feet any longer;
he looked to the heavens.
'Thank you, O Lord of Hosts,
for all the joys that I have experienced in this world.
Now, merciful God, I have the greatest need   175
that you should grant grace to my spirit,
so that my soul might journey to you,
into your dominion, Lord of angels,
travel with your protection. I entreat you
that thieves from hell should not drag it down.'   180
Then heathen slaves hacked him
and both the men who stood beside him,
Ælfnoth and Wulfmær, they both lay dead,
when they gave their lives alongside their lord.
 Then those who did not want to be there turned from the
battle: 185
the sons of Odda were the first in flight there,
Godric turned from the battle, and abandoned the brave man
who had often made him a gift of many a horse;
he leapt on the horse that his lord had owned,
onto the trappings, which was highly improper,   190
and his brothers both ran off with him,

Godwine and Godwig, they did not care for the battle,
but they turned from the fight and sought the wood,
they fled into that place of safety and saved their lives,
and more men than was at all fitting,   195
if they had all called to mind the favours
that he had done for their benefit.
Thus Offa had said to him earlier in the day
in the assembly, when he had held a meeting,
that many there spoke bravely   200
who would not hold out later in time of need.
      Then the head of the army had fallen,
Æthelred's earl. They all saw,
the companions of his hearth, that their lord lay dead.
Then proud followers pressed forward there,   205
men lacking cowardice pushed on eagerly:
they all intended then one of two things,
to lose their lives or to avenge their beloved leader.
So the son of Ælfric urged them on,
a warrior young in years, he made a speech,   210
Ælfwine then said (he spoke bravely):
'Remember the times that we often made speeches over mead,
when we raised pledges while sitting on a bench,
warriors in the hall, about fierce encounters:
now we can test who is brave.   215
I intend to make known my noble lineage to all,
that I am of a great family amongst the Mercians:
my grandfather was called Ealhhelm,
a wise and prosperous ealdorman.
Thegns will not be able to taunt me in that nation   220
that I meant to desert this militia
to seek my homeland, now that my leader lies dead,
cut to pieces in battle. That is the greatest anguish for me:
he was both my kinsman and my lord.'
Then he pressed forward, remembering his feud,   225
so that he might reach one with his spear,
a seaman in the press of the people, to lay him out on the ground,

killed with his weapon. He continued to exhort his companions
then,
his friends and comrades, that they should press forward.

     Offa made a speech, he shook his ash-spear: 230
'Indeed, Ælfwine, you have encouraged everyone,
thegns in battle. Now our lord lies dead,
the earl on the ground, it is essential for everyone
that each of us encourages the next man,
warriors at war, for as long as he is able his weapon   235
to hold and to maintain, the firm blade,
the spear and the fine sword. Us Godric has
betrayed, one and all, the cowardly son of Odda:
too many men believed, when he rode away on the horse,
on the prancing steed, that it was our lord: 240
because of that the army became fragmented here on the battlefield,
the shield-fort smashed to pieces. Blast his action,
that he should have put so many men to flight here.'
Leofsunu made a speech, and raised his shield,
his board for defence: he answered that warrior: 245
'I vow that I shall not from here
flee the length of a foot, but I intend to push forward,
to avenge my lord and friend in the struggle.
Steadfast warriors around Sturmere will have no cause
to taunt me in speech, now my beloved one is dead,   250
that I made the journey home lordless,
turned away from the fight; but a weapon must take me,
pointed spear and iron sword.' He advanced furiously incensed,
he fought strenuously, he scorned flight.
Dunnere then spoke, he shook his spear,   255
a simple yeoman, he called out over all,
he asked that each warrior should avenge Byrhtnoth:
'He must never flinch who thinks to avenge
his lord in this body of men, nor be anxious about life.'

     Then they went forward, they did not care about life;   260
the soldiers then continued fighting fiercely,
angry spear-bearers, and prayed to God

that they might avenge their beloved lord
and bring destruction on their enemies.
The hostage continued to help them eagerly;   265
he was from a brave family amongst the Northumbrians,
the son of Ecglaf, his name was Æscferth.
He did not weaken at all in the wargame;
instead he loosed forth many an arrow;
sometimes he shot into a shield, sometimes he ripped open a man;
                                                               270
every now and again he inflicted a wound
as long as he was able to wield weapons.
    Edward the Tall then still stood in the van,
ready and eager; he announced vauntingly
that he did not intend to run away by so much as a foot of land,275
to turn back, when his superior lay dead.
He broke through the shield-wall and fought against the warriors,
until he, on those seamen, his treasure-giving lord
nobly avenged, before he lay amongst the slain.
Æthelric did likewise, the noble companion,   280
eager and anxious to press forward, he fought determinedly,
Sibyrht's brother; and very many others
split the decorated shield, they defended themselves bravely.
The rim of the shield shattered, and the body armour sang
one of the songs of terror. Then in the battle struck   285
Offa the sailor so that the latter dropped onto the earth,
and there Gadd's kinsman [= Offa] himself fell to the ground.
Offa was quickly cut to pieces in the battle,
yet he had accomplished what he had promised his lord,
as he vowed formerly to his treasure-giver   290
that they must both ride back to their dwelling,
safe into the homestead, or die amongst the Vikings,
perish with wounds on the field of slaughter.
He lay near his lord as a thegn should.
    There was a smashing of shields then. The sailors advanced 295
incensed by the battle. The spearpoint frequently penetrated
the house of life of a man fated to die. Then Wistan went forward,

the son of Thurstan, he fought against the troops.
He was the destroyer of three of them in the melee
before he, the descendant of Wigelm, lay amongst the slain.   300
There was a fierce encounter there. They stood firm,
the warriors in the fight. Soldiers expired,
weary with wounds. The dead fell to the ground.
Oswald and Eadwold all the while,
the two brothers, encouraged the troops,   305
told their friends and kinsmen in speeches
that they must hold out there in that time of need,
must use their weapons without weakening.
Byrhtwold made a speech, he raised his shield,
he was an old retainer, he shook his ash-spear;   310
he instructed the men with total self-assurance:
'The spirit must be the firmer, the heart the bolder,
courage must be the greater as our strength diminishes.
Here lies our leader all cut to pieces,
the great man in the dirt. He will have cause to mourn for ever 315
who thinks of turning away from this battlegame now.
I am advanced in years; I do not intend to leave,
but I by the side of my beloved lord,
beside that wellbeloved man, intend to lie.'
Likewise the son of Æthelgar encouraged them all,   320
Godric in the battle. Frequently he loosed a spear,
caused a dart of death to fly among the Vikings;
similarly he went first among the defenders,
he slashed and laid low, until he died in the conflict.
It was not at all that same Godric who fled the battle…   325

The poem as it has survived ends in mid-sentence as it
began. Since the battle is clearly drawing to a close, it would
seem that little has been lost from the end.

6

The Aftermath of the Battle

The battle at Maldon was the first major encounter in the second wave of Viking attacks. It led immediately to a change in Æthelred's policy, and was the start of a Danish campaign that led inexorably to a change of dynasty in England. Had it not been that the new Scandinavian dynasty, which fought to gain control of the country after 991 and succeeded in 1016, failed on the death of Harthacnut in 1042 to produce a successor,

England would not have been ruled in course of time by
Normans but would have been much more closely linked
to Denmark. The outcome of Maldon may therefore be
seen as crucial to the history of England for a number of
centuries.

Byrhtnoth took his troops into battle at Maldon against
what must have seemed to him overwhelming odds, which
poses the question why he elected to do so. Whether or
not the Vikings actually asked for tribute as the poet of
The Battle of Maldon maintains, the option of buying them
off was surely available to him. We can only assume that
the strategy did not commend itself to Byrhtnoth, who
may have felt that a military solution was essential, perhaps
because he was conscious of the threat posed by such a large
force, and historically military strength had proved its worth
in keeping the land free from invasion. The aristocracy of
late Anglo-Saxon England, like that of medieval Europe
as a whole, ruled by might. Edgar's England was reported
everywhere in the chronicles, both Latin and English, as
unwontedly peaceful, yet the *Anglo-Saxon Chronicle* E version includes under the annal for 969 a note unparalleled in
other versions which reads 'In this year King Edgar ordered
all of the Isle of Thanet to be ravaged'. This military action
was not the work of Vikings, as so often in the past, but the
king's men, and there may have been many similar incidents
which went unreported in contemporary accounts. It is
in this environment that Byrhtnoth worked and ruled. He
spent his boyhood years under the warrior kings Æthelstan
and Edmund, and he grew to seniority amongst his peers
under the formidable King Edgar. Like the kings he served,
he should be seen first and foremost as a soldier and after
that as a lawmaker and major landowner. The poet is surely
right in his portrayal of him as peremptory and dismis-
sive, even arrogant; and at one point, when the Vikings are
allowed across the ford to fight on more equal terms, the
poet offers outright criticism in the form of the Old English

word *ofermod* (line 89) of which he accuses him. No crux in the poem has excited more critical controversy than the poet's use of this term. The word as a noun occurs in only three other contexts, always meaning pernicious pride (such as that displayed by Lucifer/Satan in disobeying God), but these scattered instances prove little, given the fact that the overwhelming weight of writings surviving from the period are overtly Christian. More telling perhaps is the fact that in over a hundred instances of the same word as an adjective, it invariably means 'proud'. There have been many attempts to deny that Byrhtnoth was being criticised by the poet, by taking *ofermod* as an archaic term for 'great courage' or 'magnanimity', for example, but they are vitiated by the poet's comment in the following line that he allowed the Vikings 'too much land', a statement which must be seen as condemnatory. From a military perspective there may have been many reasons why Byrhtnoth might have wished to give ground (e.g. to entice the enemy into a situation favorable in some way to himself), but after the death of Byrhtnoth and those close to him, the reasons for his decisions are not available to us. In the event, the contemporary observer, represented for posterity by the poet, felt that the move was unwise, but these observers had the benefit of hindsight.

Having ruled Essex single-handed for thirty-five years, Byrhtnoth was, in effect, a king. While his loyalty to the West-Saxon crown cannot be doubted, his power in his own realm was absolute. With his length of service it is easy to see why he should have been given whatever suzerainty over Northumbria he had. It is also easy to understand why he could not contemplate allowing an invader to enter his land unopposed. He should be seen in the mould of King Alfred and as a predecessor of Harold at Stamford Bridge and Hastings seventy-five years after he himself fell. His duty was to defend his kingdom whatever the cost. Even heavily outnumbered and with little chance of achieving an easy victory, he clearly had something to gain by bringing the

Vikings to battle, and that was to reduce the Viking numbers radically and thus to limit the damage they could do. There are many examples in European history of a chance happening on the battlefield bringing about an unexpected change of fortune. Alfred and his brother King Æthelred, for example, had a number of encounters in 871, such as their fight at the unlocated *Meretun* when the English were winning throughout the day, but the Danes for reasons now lost were victorious at nightfall. The chance breaking of the English ranks at Hastings can be seen as a similar unexpected turning of the tide. Events closely parallel to those at Maldon occurred, moreover, at the battle of Brissarthe in 866 when the Franks had a Viking army trapped and unable to reach their boats, until their leaders, Count Robert of Anjou and Blois and Duke Ramnulf of Aquitaine, were killed, at which point the Frankish army turned for home and the Vikings were able to escape. This battle also offers a prime example of the fact that the death of leaders in medieval warfare often had a catastrophic effect on morale. Byrhtnoth would undoubtedly have been as aware as the Vikings of the importance to the latter of not being cut off from their boats by the tide. Although he was outnumbered at the start of the battle, he may well have had a strategy beyond that of simply damage on the enemy. Reinforcements might already have been organised, for example, by land or by sea. Because of lack of documentary evidence and in particular the mutilated state of the poem from which so much of our information derives, there is no means of knowing whether any wider strategy was in place. But even if the aim was solely to disable the invaders sufficiently to stop their predations, that aim might well have succeeded had the English line held – and the fact that it did not was the result, according to the poet, of the death of Byrhtnoth, and in that the poet was undoubtedly right.

After the battle was over, the *Liber Eliensis* states that the abbot and monks from the abbey at Ely collected Byrhtnoth's body and buried it 'with honour' in their minster. It also notes that the Vikings had carried off his head as a trophy, and that when Byrhtnoth was buried, his head was replaced by a ball of wax. Since the Anglo-Saxon church at Ely was pulled down in the twelfth century when a much larger Norman one was built, it is not possible to determine what the phrase 'with honour' means, whether the burial was before the high altar or in a side wall or chapel. There is no doubt, however, about the subsequent fate of his remains. His body, still with the ball of wax for the head as an identifier, was translated to the north wall of the choir of the Norman church in 1154 along with those of six other major Anglo-Saxon benefactors of the monastery. The remains were moved again in 1322 when part of the Norman church collapsed, and they were finally removed to their present position in the eighteenth century when considerable modifications were made to the church, by then the cathedral seat of the bishop of Ely, the monastery having been dissolved under Henry VIII. Fortunately, detailed records of the medieval tombs were made at the time of their removal in the eighteenth century, showing that they were marked by drawings of their occupants, although these are of limited value in that they are in the style of the fourteenth rather than the tenth century (see Plate 54). Thus they are of interest only in the perspective that they offer on the late medieval understanding of early figures in the church's history. Of somewhat greater interest is the fact that the drawings show the names of the dead above their tombs, exhibiting the continuity of the marking of the graves throughout the medieval period. The records, including the drawings, were published in an eighteenth-century monograph by James Bentham, an Ely prebend who had antiquarian interests. He pays particular attention to Byrhtnoth's body, noting that the head was missing and giving the size of the leg and arm bones so that the stature of the deceased could be reckoned. Byrhtnoth's height was calculated at six feet nine inches, but it has been demonstrated in modern times that the length of the foot is included in the reckoning, and it is probably safer to assume that he was just over six feet in height, only slightly taller than the average nobleman of the period. In the eighteenth-century translation of the corpse, Byrhtnoth's remains and those of the six churchmen buried alongside him were moved to the Bishop West chapel at the extreme south-east corner of the church, where they rest today (Plate 56). They are now within seven separate niches, each marked with the name of the incumbent, Byrhtnoth's tomb identifying him as Duke of Northumbria, killed in battle against the Danes in 991 (Plate 57).

The *Liber Eliensis* has one further item of note. It cites a list of gifts which Byrhtnoth's widow gave to Ely in his memory after his death, which, together with estates and a gold torque, includes a hanging, embroidered with her husband's deeds. It is likely that this hanging was an embroidery depicting the battle similar to the Bayeux Tapestry with its representation of the battle of Hastings (the Bayeux Tapestry itself being an embroidery rather than a tapestry), though it may have included Byrhtnoth's earlier deeds. It has been suggested that it was only the earlier heroic encounters against Viking invaders that were depicted because the *Liber Eliensis* states that the gifts were made 'at the time that her husband was killed and buried', but this idea can be safely discounted on the grounds that the nobleman's widow would certainly have wished to commemorate his last stand. Given that the *Liber Eliensis* dates from the later twelfth century, 'at the time' might be any time before Ælfflæd's own death in 1002. The weaving of an embroidery in Byrhtnoth's memory is not unexpected. It was the custom in noble houses until comparatively recent times for the lady of the house and her maids to employ themselves with needlework. English needlework was very highly prized throughout Europe in the Anglo-Saxon period, and it is not surprising to find that English needlewomen were commissioned soon after the

Norman Conquest to produce an extended account of the battle of Hastings for Bishop Odo of Bayeux. Manuscript illuminations throughout the period indicate how such hangings were used, showing them positioned behind furniture and over doorways to eliminate draughts (Plate 58). In late Anglo-Saxon England every house had a loom, however rudimentary, for the making of textiles, and all noble houses would have had the leisure and wealth necessary for the design and construction of large-scale hangings, as well as the need to provide for the comfort of both master and guests. The scale of the Byrhtnoth embroidery can only be guessed at, but its representation of Byrhtnoth's deeds implies that it was far from small. The information that it was made is important to historians in that it is the only evidence that survives that 'tapestries' such as Bayeux were, if not commonplace, then certainly not unique. The *Liber Eliensis* gives no indication that the hanging survived to the 1170s when the book was compiled, but it may well have been in existence when the account on which the *Liber Eliensis* drew was composed, and the author's misunderstanding of the tapestry may account for the assertion that two battles rather than one took place at Maldon. More broadly, two major points may be deduced from the creation of the embroidery: first that Byrhtnoth's life was seen to be sufficiently significant to require a visual record, and that such a record of their principal benefactor would be welcome to the contemporary community at Ely, and second that works of art dealing with the Danish incursion are not restricted to the single poem that survives.

Byrhtnoth's death was a national and also a local event, proclaimed by his family in the embroidery and the other gifts to Ely, celebrated in the commissioning of a poem on his death by an unknown person or persons (perhaps members of his family or friends such as Ealdorman Æthelwine of East Anglia), observed in the prayers of monastic communities as far apart as Ely and Winchester, and preserved for posterity in all copies of the *Anglo-Saxon Chronicle* which include entries for the 990s, as well as in the Latin chronicle tradition which is found throughout the Norman period. In other words, the death of Byrhtnoth continued to resonate in later ages, and thanks to the survival of the Old English poem, it continues to be of interest today. But the implications of the English defeat at the battle of Maldon have not always been fully understood, as the encounter is frequently seen as a minor conflict by comparison with King Alfred's long struggle against the Vikings or with King Harold's battles with northmen and Normans in 1066. Yet just as Alfred's victory over the Vikings at Edington in 878 led ultimately to the formation of England as a single political unit, so Ealdorman Byrhtnoth's defeat at Maldon led inexorably to the subjection of England as a whole to a Danish conqueror, and at a later date to the submission of the country to a Norman one. The united state of Anglo-Saxon England was formed as a result of one battle in 878 and destroyed two centuries later by another, but, though its destruction literally took place at Hastings in 1066, its seeds lay in the fight on the shores of Essex in 991.

With the exception of the *Liber Eliensis* report that the Vikings sailed off with Byrhtnoth's head after the battle as a trophy, chronicles of the period give no indication of what happened immediately after the encounter. We do know, however, that the Vikings were paid off later in the summer. Versions CDE of the *Anglo-Saxon Chronicle* note that the invaders were paid tribute that year on the advice of Archbishop Sigeric for the first time, to the sum of ten thousand pounds, 'because of the great damage that they were doing along the sea coast'. Since Sigeric was archbishop of Canterbury, and his church had considerable property in Kent, it might be supposed that the Vikings crossed into Kent after leaving Maldon and continued ravaging there, but this supposition is undermined by the fact that the church had property in every part of the realm, and the tribute was raised through a system of universal taxation on land that included the extensive church lands. The significant point here is that the Vikings who defeated Byrhtnoth were still sufficiently strong after the battle to pose a threat great enough to be worth a very large sum in tribute. In the words of the poet John Milton in his *History of Britain*, published in 1670, 'it was thought best for the present to buy that with Silver which they could not gain with their Iron'. Earlier chapters of this book have traced the depredations of what must be supposed to have been the same army in England in subsequent years, and for the rest of Æthelred's reign that army continued to be dangerous enough to warrant the payment of huge sums, amounting in all to almost a quarter of a million pounds in silver by 1014. These figures, drawn from documentary sources, can be tested by reference to the hoards of silver found in Scandinavian deposits, which in turn can be dated by the coins of which they are largely made up. If all the finds from Iceland, Norway, Denmark, Sweden and the Slav lands are taken into account, tens of millions of English coins were exported to Scandinavia during this period, some no doubt through trade but the vast majority in tribute.

The ensuing Viking attacks of the second phase may be summarized as follows. As noted above, it is as certain as it is possible to be at this distance that Swein Forkbeard, king of Denmark, was the leader of the attack on Maldon in 991 and that he remained responsible for subsequent attacks on English shores in the early 990s. There is conclusive evidence that he was in England in 994, but he then disappears from the English arena and was undoubtedly back in Denmark in the last years of the millennium, wresting control of Norway from Olaf Tryggvason, his former comrade-in-arms, thanks to the diplomacy of King Æthelred which was directed towards dividing the Viking leaders in order not to be conquered by them. By 1000 Swein had overlordship of Norway as well as command of Denmark and turned his eyes once again towards England. Meantime, in England a Viking army, presumably commanded by Swein's subordinates, ranged in 997 over Devon, Cornwall and (South) Wales, initiating a campaign that lasted through the next two years. In 1000 they sailed to Normandy but returned the following year and in 1002 the English bought them off with twenty-four thousand pounds. In that same year, Æthelred's diplomacy led him into his closest tie yet with Normandy when he embarked upon a second marriage with Duke Richard of Normandy's sister. The aim was to ensure that the Vikings lacked a base in Normandy from which to attack England, but the ultimate effect was to introduce Norman influence into English affairs. In 1003, the Vikings, despite the tribute that they had been paid the previous year, were ravaging southern England again, and for the first time for some years the *Chronicle* mentions Swein at the head of these invaders. It is possible that he invaded because his sister Gunnhild is reported to have been killed in the St Brice's Day massacre ordered by Æthelred against all Danes living in England because of a supposed plot against him, but it is more likely that Swein's ambition to conquer England was wider than that. He continued to lead the Viking forces in England for the whole of the next year, but in 1005 the harvest failed and the ensuing famine drove the Vikings back to Denmark. The army returned the following year, however, and remained in England subsequently for a prolonged period, until an attack on Canterbury in 1011 in which Archbishop Ælfheah was captured and later murdered. This event served to divide the Vikings, and forty-five ships transferred their allegiance to Æthelred, but their defection appears to have had little impact on Swein's strength. In 1013 he sailed north to the Humber and along the Trent, and was accepted as king first by the Northumbrians and then by the ealdormen and earls of the north-east midlands, and soon afterwards, as the chronicler reports, he had secured hostages from every shire north of Watling Street. Effectively he ruled all the areas assigned to Danes in the settlement made by Alfred in 878. When he crossed Watling Street and began campaigning in the south, the towns and shires submitted to him one after another, beginning with Oxford and Winchester itself. Only London held out against him, because King Æthelred was garrisoned there with his fleet, but even London could not withstand him indefinitely when the rest of the country had submitted to him. Recognising his weakness, Æthelred sent his queen and sons to Normandy, while he remained uneasily in England until Christmas 1013, having retreated from London to the Isle of Wight. Finally he too sailed for Normandy and exile, and Swein ruled England.

But Fortune is fickle. On 2 February 1014, Swein died, and after protracted negotiations, Æthelred returned to England during Lent. Swein's eldest surviving son Cnut was accepted by the Danish army as king but he needed to return to Denmark to secure his position there. But before he could do so, he found himself forced onto the defensive – an unfamiliar experience by that date for the Danes. Æthelred, reinvigorated by his return to power, successfully attacked Cnut in Lincolnshire and forced him to put to sea with his fleet. On his way to Denmark, however, Cnut put in to Sandwich and set ashore all the hostages that had been given to his father, having first cut off their hands and noses. The action constituted notice of his future conduct towards the English. The respite afforded by his departure was short-lived. In 1015 he returned England, and both then and in the following year fought pitched battles against Æthelred's son and heir, Edmund Ironside. On 23 April 1016 King Æthelred died, and Edmund was elected king, but Cnut was still a potent threat, and the fighting continued up and down the kingdom as the two armies chased each other and fought, wreaking havoc on the entire population. Finally, after a particularly bloody battle at *Assandun* (either Ashingdon or Ashdon) in Essex, Edmund was soundly defeated. He and Cnut reached an agreement whereby England was divided between them along the lines of the Alfredian division, until on 30 November Edmund suddenly and unexpectedly died. Cnut was accepted as king of all England.

Cnut ruled until 1035 and was succeeded by two sons, half-brothers, Harold Harefoot and Harthacnut, but neither of them had issue and the Danish line, as noted above, ran out in 1042. The English nobles then turned back to the offspring of Æthelred, to Edward, known as the Confessor, a child of his second marriage to Emma of Normandy, who had been in that country since Æthelred's exile in 1014, and Edward then ruled until 1066. Viking control of England thus ended forever in 1042. In its place, Norman influence grew, culminating with the defeat of Harold at Hastings on 14 October 1066. Sturmer, the village on the Cambridgeshire border of Essex where the man known in Old English as Leofsunu had once farmed his land, still had two free-born tenants in 1066, a man and a woman, but by 1086 both manors had passed, along with six others in Essex, to Tihel the Breton for services rendered to William at the battle of Hastings.

Further Reading

In general, works in this section are books rather than essays in learned periodicals. For up-to-date academic essays on particular subjects, the reader is referred especially to the annual periodical *Anglo-Saxon England*, published by Cambridge University Press. In each issue, the latter also has a list of publications on Anglo-Saxon subjects for the previous year, divided into categories such as Literature, History and Archaeology, which anyone wishing to follow up particular topics will find helpful. A useful full list can be found in Simon Keynes, *Anglo-Saxon England: A Bibliographical Handbook for Students of Anglo-Saxon History*, 2nd ed., Anglo-Saxon, Norse and Celtic Guides, Texts and Studies 1 (Cambridge, 2001).

Chapter 1

The standard history of the Anglo-Saxons is F.M. Stenton, *Anglo-Saxon England*, The Oxford History of England vol. II, 3rd ed. (Oxford, 1971), a full, immensely learned and precise account of the whole Anglo-Saxon period based on historical sources, with the benefit of a detailed index for easy reference. It may be supplemented by Dorothy Whitelock, *The Beginnings of English Society*, The Pelican History of England vol. 2 (Harmondsworth, 1952, revised ed. 1977), which offers a sensible, easily digested survey again of the whole of the pre-Conquest period; P. Hunter Blair, *An Introduction to Anglo-Saxon England*, 2nd ed. (Cambridge, 1977), which covers the period by subject rather than chronologically as in Stenton; J. Campbell, E. John and P. Wormald, *The Anglo-Saxons* (Oxford, 1982, reprinted by Penguin Books, 1991), which is a lavishly illustrated account of the period; and David Hill, *An Atlas of Anglo-Saxon England* (Oxford, 1981), which gives a brilliant evocation of the history of England before the Norman Conquest through a wide range of maps, diagrams and statistics drawn from the historical sources. Information about a vast array of individuals and particular subjects can be found in *The Blackwell Encyclopedia of Anglo-Saxon England*, ed. Michael Lapidge, John Blair, Simon Keynes and Donald Scragg (Oxford, 1999), and, more widely across the medieval period, in *Medieval England, An Encyclopedia*, ed. Paul E. Szarmach, M. Teresa Tavormina and Joel T. Rosenthal (New York and London, 1998). Many of the primary sources, both Latin and Old English, are translated in *English Historical Documents*, gnl. ed. David C. Douglas, vol. I: *c.*500-1042, ed. Dorothy Whitelock (London, 1955, with a greatly expanded 2nd ed., London, 1979), an indispensible treasure-house of material.

There are many general histories of Anglo-Saxon England to choose from, including, in order of publication, R. H. Hodgkin, *History of the Anglo-Saxons*, 3rd ed., 2 vols. (Oxford, 1953); H. R. Loyn, *Anglo-Saxon England and the*

Norman Conquest, 2nd ed. (London and New York, 1962); C. Brooke, *The Saxon and Norman Kings* (London, 1963, 3rd ed. London, 2001), H. P. R. Finberg, *The Formation of England 550 – 1042* (London, 1974), P. H. Sawyer, *From Roman Britain to Norman England* (London, 1978), David Wilson, *The Anglo-Saxons,* 3rd ed., Pelican Books, concentrating on archaeology (Harmondsworth, 1981), C. Oman, *A History of England before the Norman Conquest* (London, 1994). All have their strengths and all have individual approaches to the period. A fine, superbly illustrated account of the early period is to be found in the catalogue to a British Museum exhibition, *The Making of England: Anglo-Saxon Art and Culture AD 600-900* (London, 1991). The exhibition was a companion one to a British Museum one which covered the later period and again its catalogue is useful: *The Golden Age of Anglo-Saxon Art 966-1066,* ed. Janet Backhouse, D. H. Turner and Leslie Webster (London, 1984). Two collections of specialised studies with much material on the later Anglo-Saxon period are Eric John, *Orbis Britanniae and other Studies* (Leicester, 1966), and James Campbell, *The Anglo-Saxon State* (London and New York, 2000).

There are also many more general studies of specific areas of interest, a few of which can be mentioned to broaden the range of information offered by the general histories. H. P. R. Finberg, 'Anglo-Saxon England to 1042', *The Agrarian History of England and Wales,* vol. I.ii (Cambridge, 1972), offers a very full account of farming, the animals raised, and general rural development in Anglo-Saxon times, with more up-to-date information in some respects in Peter Fowler, *Farming in the First Millennium: British Agriculture between Julius Caesar and William the Conqueror* (Cambridge, 2002); Della Hooke, *The Landscape of Anglo-Saxon England* (London and New York, 1998), is a wide-ranging account of the countryside and activities in it; Albert C. Leighton, *Transport and Communication in Early Medieval Europe AD 500-1100* (Newton Abbot, 1972), is a very generalised but readable account of a neglected subject; Patrick Wormald, *The Making of English Law: King Alfred to the Twelfth Century*, I: Legislation and its Limits (Oxford, 1999), is a magisterial book concentrating on the texts but saying a great deal about the law generally and the kings that made it (the laws themselves may be found translated in F. Attenborough, *The Laws of the Earliest English Kings*, Cambridge, 1922); the range of essays by different experts in their fields on a variety of subjects in *The Archaeology of Anglo-Saxon England*, ed. David M. Wilson (London, 1976), with plates and a great many drawings, as well as a gazetteer of settlements; H. M. Taylor and Joan Taylor, *Anglo-Saxon Architecture*, 3 vols. (Cambridge, 1965–1978); and finally a group with titles which speak for themselves: Ronald Jessup, *Anglo-Saxon Jewellery* (London, 1950); David M. Wilson, *Anglo-Saxon Art from the Seventh Century to the Norman Conquest* (London, 1984); S. Crawford, *Childhood in Anglo-Saxon England* (Stroud, Glos., 1999), *The Year 1000: Medical Practice at the End of the First Millennium*, ed. Peregrine Horden and Emilie Savage-Smith, *Social History of Medicine* 13.2 (2000), Gale R. Owen-Crocker, *Dress in Anglo-Saxon England* (Manchester, 1986, 2nd expanded ed., Cambridge 2005).

Many publications deal specifically with the *Anglo-Saxon Chronicle*, ranging from translations of either one version or many, to detailed studies of the text and notes on it. The most up-to-date and scholarly editions of the texts, with close examination of each manuscript version, may be found in a collaborative edition currently in progress, with each of the main texts having now been published. As a whole, the edition is called *The Anglo-Saxon Chronicle: A Collaborative Edition*, the relevant individual volumes of the versions referred to in this book being vol. 3: *MS A*, ed. J. M. Bately (Cambridge, 1983); vol. 4: *MS B*, ed. Simon Taylor (Cambridge, 1983); vol. 5: *MS C*, ed. Katherine O'Brien O'Keeffe (Cambridge, 2001); vol. 6: *MS D*, ed. G. P. Cubbin (Cambridge, 1996); and vol. 7: *MS E*, ed. Susan

Irvine (Cambridge, 2004). For translations of all of the ver-
sions (except where they are identical with one another), see
The Anglo-Saxon Chronicle, trans. with an introduction by G.
N. Garmondsway, Everyman's Library vol. 624 (London and
New York, 1953, rev. ed. 1960). There are many other modern
translations, e.g. M. Swanton, *The Anglo-Saxon Chronicle*
(London, 1996), concentrating on the E version, while an
older one, but still useful, is *The Anglo-Saxon Chronicle: A
Revised Translation*, ed. D. Whitelock, with D. C. Douglas and
S. I. Tucker, 2nd impression (London, 1965). The manuscript
of version A of the *Chronicle* has been printed in facsimile
in *The Parker Chronicle and Laws: a Facsimile Edition*, ed. R.
Flower and H. Smith, Early English Text Society, original
series 28 (London, 1941, repr. 1973)

On King Alfred, the best introduction is to be found
in *Alfred the Great: Asser's Life of King Alfred and other
Contemporary Sources*, trans. S. Keynes and M. Lapidge,
Penguin Books (Harmondsworth, 1983). General accounts
are numerous; among the more recent (taking account of
the most up-to-date scholarship) are two: Alfred Smyth,
King Alfred the Great (Oxford, 1995), which offers a contro-
versial view of the evidence surviving for the history of the
reign, and Richard Abels, *Alfred the Great: War, Kingship and
Culture in Anglo-Saxon England*, The Medieval World Series
(Harlow, 1998), which sticks to the traditional line. On the
following reign, see especially *Edward the Elder 899-924*, ed.
N. J. Higham and D. H. Hill (London, 2001). Specific to
Alfred's and his successors' building of the burhs is an excel-
lent series of papers in *The Defence of Wessex: the Burghal
Hidage and Anglo-Saxon Fortifications*, ed. David Hill and
Alexander R. Rumble (Manchester, 1996).

The background within the British Isles is the subject of
many of the essays in *From the Vikings to the Normans*, ed.
Wendy Davies (Oxford, 2003). The continental background
is considered in *The Rebirth of Towns in the West, A.D. 700–
1050*, ed. R. Hodges and B. Hobley, British Archaeological

Reports 68 (Oxford, 1968), J. M. Wallace-Hadrill, *Early Germanic Kingship in England and on the Continent* (Oxford, 1971), D. A. Bullough, *The Age of Charlemagne* (London, 1973), and *The New Cambridge Medieval History,* ed. Paul Fouracre: esp. vol. II, *c. 700–c. 900,* ed. Rosamond McKitterick (Cambridge, 1995), and vol. III *c. 900–c. 1024,* ed. Timothy Reuter (Cambridge, 1999). See also the appropriate essays in *Ideal and Reality in Frankish and Anglo-Saxon Society: Studies presented to J. M. Wallace-Hadrill,* ed. Patrick Wormald, Donald Bullough and Roger Collins (Oxford, 1983), J. L. Nelson, *Politics and Ritual in Early Medieval Europe* (London, 1986), and *People and Places in Northern Europe 500-1600: Essays in Honour of Peter Hayes Sawyer,* ed. I. Wood and N. Lund (Woodbridge, Suffolk, 1991).

Chapter 2

The principal and very recent study of the ships is *The Skuldelev Ships I,* ed. Ole Crumlin-Pedersen and Olaf Olsen, Ships and Boats of the North vol. 4, (Roskilde, 2002), which is a very full account of the excavation and preservation of the five Skuldelev wrecks, with detailed analysis of the history surrounding their building and use, as these can be deduced from the remains. It also puts the Skuldelev ships into the wider context of ship-building in the later Viking age. A second volume is expected soon. Other works, published before this, now offer material relating to Viking ships which is slightly out-of-date in some details, but they remain useful in that many of their accounts are readable and set the material into different contexts. Such are: *Medieval Scandinavia: An Encyclopedia,* ed. P. Pulsiano (New York and London, 1993), and the general histories of the Vikings listed in the next section.

The *Encomium Emmae Reginae,* which, as well as offering information on Viking boats, has much to say about the politics of the eleventh century, was edited and translated by A. Campbell in the Camden 3rd series (London, 1949), now re-issued by the Royal Historical Society with a long and full introduction by Simon Keynes (Cambridge, 1998). Readers who prefer a more imaginative narrative style might try Harriet O'Brien, *Queen Emma and the Vikings: A History of Power, Love and Greed in Eleventh-Century England* (London, 2005).

Chapter 3

The best two modern introductions to the Viking Age are *The Oxford Illustrated History of the Vikings*, ed. Peter Sawyer (Oxford, 1997), and John Haywood, *Encyclopedia of the Viking Age* (London, 2000). A good general account of Viking activity everywhere is P. H. Sawyer, *The Age of the Vikings*, 2nd ed. (London, 1971). Among the very great range of books on the subject should be mentioned (in order of publication): H.R. Loyn, *The Vikings in Britain* (London, 1977), Gwyn Jones, *A History of the Vikings* (London, 1984), E. Roesdahl, *The Vikings*, Penguin Books (Harmondsworth, 1992), M.K. Lawson, *The Danes in England in the Early Eleventh Century* (London, 1993), P. Sawyer, *Kings and Vikings: Scandinavia and Europe AD 700–1100* (New York, 1994), P. Cavill, *The Vikings: Fear and Faith* (London, 2001). There are also some pertinent essays in *Anglo-Scandinavian England: Norse-English Relations in the Period before the Conquest*, ed. John D. Niles and Mark Amodio, (New York, 1989), and *The Scandinavians from the Vendel Period to the Tenth Century*, ed. Judith Jesch (Woodbridge, Suffolk, 2002), while a useful well illustrated catalogue of the Viking exhibition held in Denmark, York and London in 1981/1982 is *The Vikings in England and in their Danish Homeland*, ed. E. Roesdahl, J. Graham-Campbell, P. Connor and K. Pearson (London, 1982). See also J.A. Graham-Campbell, *Viking Artefacts* (London 1980).

There are many studies of the important developments in late Anglo-Saxon coinage, in particular of King Edgar's reform of the monetary system and of Anglo-Saxon coins in Viking hoards. The best introduction is in *Medieval European Coinage I: Early Middle Ages (5ᵗʰ–10ᵗʰ Centuries)*, ed. P. Grierson and M. Blackburn (Cambridge, 1986), but the interested reader should also refer to H.B.A. Petersson, *Anglo-Saxon Currency: King Edgar's Reform to the Norman Conquest* (Lund, 1969), to the essays in *Anglo-Saxon Coins*, ed. R.H.M. Dolley (London, 1961), and also to C.E. Blunt, B.H.I.H. Stewart and C. S. S. Lyon, *Coinage in Tenth-Century England* (Oxford, 1989), and the massively detailed account of Scandinavian hoards in Kenneth Jonsson, *The New Era: The Reformation of the Late Anglo-Saxon Coinage* (Stockholm, 1987).

Chapter 4

The late Anglo-Saxon period is fully covered in most of the books listed under Chapter 1, but there are also some works relating specifically to the late period, in particular to the reign of Æthelred, foremost among them being Simon Keynes, *The Diplomas of King Æthelred 'the Unready' 978–1016: A Study in their Use as Historical Evidence* (Cambridge, 1980). A readable account of the reign may be found in Ryan Lavelle, *Æthelred II: King of the English, 978–1016* (Stroud, Glos., 2002). Also extremely valuable are the essays in *Ethelred the Unready: Papers from the Millenary Conference*, ed. D. Hill, British Archaeological Reports, British series 59 (Oxford, 1978). Of prime cartographic importance is the Ordnance Survey *Britain before the Norman Conquest 871 AD to 1066* (Southampton, 1973), which has a brief historical background to the whole period, as well as a gazetteer of places mentioned. The South Sheet map (broadly England and Wales) is of particular importance to the the late Anglo-Saxon period, offering details of churches by period, place-names which give evidence of settlement, and significant roads.

The archaeology and history of towns have been the subject of many studies, most notably *The Cambridge Urban History of Britain*, vol. I: *600–1540*, ed. D.M. Palliser (Cambridge, 2000).

Also to be recommended are S. Reynolds, *An Introduction to the History of Medieval Towns* (Oxford, 1977), and *Anglo-Saxon Towns in Southern England*, ed. J. Haslam (Chichester, 1984), and relevant essays in *The Rebirth of Towns in the West*, ed. R. Hodges and B. Hobley (London, 1988).

Domesday Book has naturally attracted a great deal of attention, and there is a wealth of literature associated with it, some of it quite old but no less valuable for that. Texts and documents concerning the creation of the book itself are available in translation in *English Historical Documents*, gnl. ed. David C. Douglas, vol. II: 1042–1189, ed. David C. Douglas and George W. Greenaway, 2nd ed. (London, 1981), pp.911 ff. There is also a good general introduction to the survey in the introduction, pp.858 ff. The basic general book on the detail of the survey remains the two volumes of Sir Henry Ellis, *A General Introduction to Domesday Book*, Public Records Commission (London, 1833, repr. in facsimile, Trowbridge and London, 1971), which is particularly valuable for its wealth of indexes. Ellis's work formed an introduction to a typographical facsimile of Domesday made under the editorship of Abraham Farley with type specially created for the purpose at the end of the eighteenth century with government funds reported to be in the region of £38,000. The facsimile has been reproduced, shire by shire, in a multi-volume photographic edition with facing translation by the Phillimore press: *Domesday Book*, ed. John Morris (Chichester, 1975–present, all volumes currently still available). Volume 32, 'Essex', edited by Alexander Rumble, was drawn upon extensively for the Prologue of this book. Penguin Books also have made available a complete translation of Domesday Book, by Ann Williams and Geoffrey Martin (repr. Harmondsworth, 1992). Among other general books on the subject should be mentioned: V.H. Galbraith, *The Making of Domesday Book* (Oxford, 1961), R. Welldon Fell, *An Introduction to Domesday Book* (London, 1963), *Domesday Book: A Reassessment*, ed. P. Sawyer (London,

1985), and, for a full list of studies, D. Bates, *A Bibliography of Domesday Book* (Woodbridge, S Suffolk, 1986). On Essex, see now *Little Domesday Book: Essex*, ed. Ann Williams and Geoffrey Martin, 2 vols. (London, 2000).

Chapter 5

The most important books on warfare in England during the period are C. Warren Hollister, *Anglo-Saxon Military Institutions on the Eve of the Norman Conquest* (Oxford, 1962), and Richard P. Abels, *Lordship and Military Obligation in Anglo-Saxon England* (London, 1988), which has a very full bibliography. Weaponry is discussed by a number of scholars. Books on archaeology listed above all have accounts of weapons. The fullest discussion of the sword is in H.R. Ellis-Davidson, *The Sword in Anglo-Saxon England* (Oxford, 1962), and of the spear in M.J. Swanton, *The Spearheads of the Anglo-Saxon Settlements* (London, 1973). More references can be found in the appropriate chapters of Everett U. Crosby, *Medieval Warfare: A Bibliographical Guide* (New York, 2000), and Kelly DeVries, *A Cumulative Bibliography of Medieval Military History and Technology* (Leiden, 2002).

The definitive edition of the poem remains *The Battle of Maldon*, ed. D. G. Scragg (Manchester, 1981), although the introduction needs revision in a few respects in the light of more recent scholarship. The edition which it replaced is still useful in many respects: *The Battle of Maldon*, ed. E.V. Gordon (London, 1937, repr. with a supplement by D. G. Scragg, Manchester, 1976). The poem has for many years been one the foremost items in the Old English literary canon and consequently the volume of critical studies on it is both already large and increasing annually. Amongst the best essays are those to be found in two collections which marked the one thousandth anniversary of the battle: *The Battle of Maldon A.D. 991*, ed. Donald Scragg (Oxford, 1991), which includes a complete bibliography of studies on the poem to 1990, and *The Battle of Maldon: Fiction and Fact*, ed.

Janet Cooper (London, 1993). The account of the battle and its repercussions in this book has drawn heavily upon the research published in these volumes. The tide times used in Chapter 5 were estimated again at the time that the battle was in the forefront of public imagination in the millenary year of 1991, in David Cartwright and Charles Abbott Conway, 'Maldon and the Tides', *The Cambridge Review* 112 (December 1991), 180-3.

Texts and translations of the relevant sections of the Ely and Ramsey Chronicles, as well as of the obits, can be found in *The Battle of Maldon A.D. 991*, ed. Scragg. For fuller information, see *Liber Eliensis*, ed. E. O. Blake, Camden 3rd series (London, 1962).

Chapter 6
Specifically on the eleventh-century Danish kings of England, see Ian Howard, *Swein Forkbeard's Invasions and the Danish Conquest of England, 991–1017* (Woodbridge, Suffolk, 2003), *The Reign of Cnut, King of England, Denmark and Norway*, ed. Alexander R. Rumble (Leicester, 1994), and M. K. Lawson, *Cnut: The Danes in England in the Early Eleventh Century* (London, 1995).

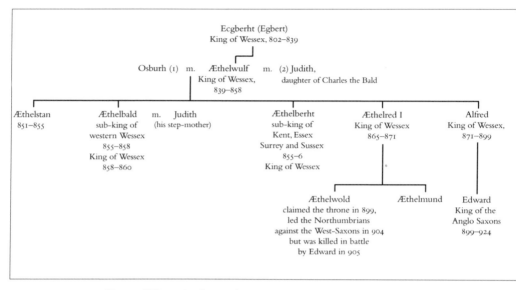

66. Kings of Wessex in the ninth century

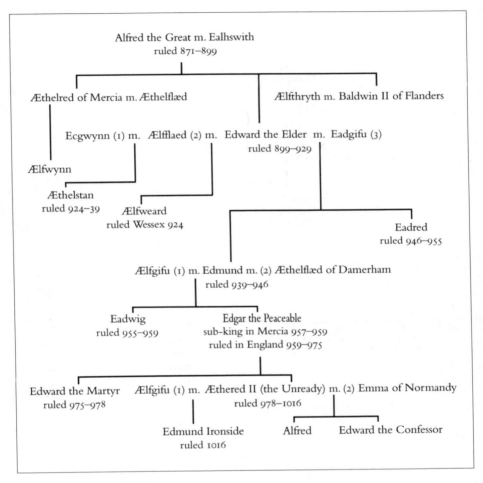

67. The house of Alfred

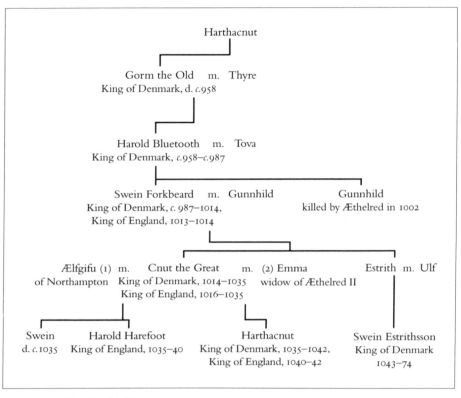

Harthacnut

Gorm the Old   m.   Thyre
King of Denmark, d. *c.*958

Harold Bluetooth   m.   Tova
King of Denmark, *c.*958–*c.*987

Swein Forkbeard   m.   Gunnhild   Gunnhild
King of Denmark, *c.* 987–1014,   killed by Æthelred in 1002
King of England, 1013–1014

Ælfgifu (1) m.   Cnut the Great   m. (2) Emma   Estrith m. Ulf
of Northampton King of Denmark, 1014–1035   widow of Æthelred II

Swein   Harold Harefoot   Harthacnut   Swein Estrithsson
d. *c.*1035   King of England, 1035–40   King of Denmark, 1035–1042,   King of Denmark
                King of England, 1040–42   1043–74

68. The Danish kings

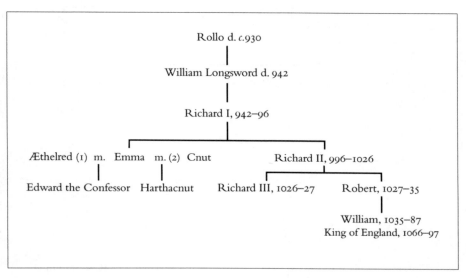

69. Dukes of Normandy

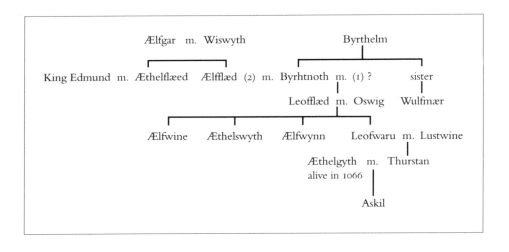

Ælfgar m. Wiswyth   Byrthelm

King Edmund m. Æthelflæed   Ælfflæd (2) m. Byrhtnoth m. (1) ?   sister

Leofflæd m. Oswig   Wulfmær

Ælfwine   Æthelswyth   Ælfwynn   Leofwaru m. Lustwine

Æthelgyth m. Thurstan
alive in 1066

Askil

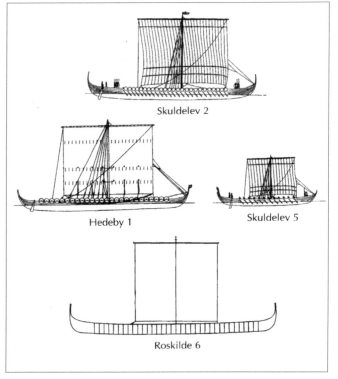

Skuldelev 2

Hedeby 1

Skuldelev 5

Roskilde 6

70. *Above:* Byrhtnoth's family

71. *Left:* Relative sizes of the longships. Drawing Morten Göthsche © The Vikingship Museum, Denmark

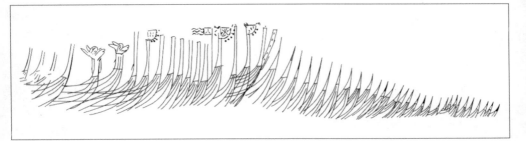

72. Drawing of the Bergen stick etching (see Plate 10). © Museum of Cultural History – University of Oslo, Norway

	lines 1-5 entries for annals 984-988
	line 6, annal numbers 989-992 written across the line
	lines 7-10, annal for 993 written over the erased annal numbers 990-993
continuation of the annal for 993 in the margin of lines 11-13 late addition in margin of lines 13-15	lines 11-17 annals 994-1000, largely empty
	lines 18-25m long annal for 1001

73. Plan of the A chronicle, fol. 129 verso (see Plate 38)

List of Illustrations

Plates

9. Visitors enjoying a reconstructed Skuldelev boat at sea. Photographer Werner Karrasch © The Vikingship Museum, Denmark.

10. Etched stick from Bergen, Norway. Photo courtesy of the Bergen University Museum, Norway.

11 and 12. Silver penny from King Edgar's reign. Photograph: Mark Blackburn.

13 and 14. Edgar's reformed coinage. Photograph: Mark Blackburn.

15 and 16. Æthelred's first coinage. Photograph: Mark Blackburn.

17. Quartered and halved pennies. Photograph: Mark Blackburn.

18 and 19. Æthelred's Second Hand penny. Photograph: Mark Blackburn.

20 and 21. Æthelred's Hand of God penny. Photograph: Mark Blackburn.

22 and 23. The 'Helmet' penny. Photograph: Mark Blackburn.

24 and 25 Æthelred's Agnus Dei penny. Photograph: Mark Blackburn.

26 and 27. Æthelred's Last Small Cross. Photograph: Mark Blackburn.

28 and 29. Æthelred's Crux penny. Photograph: Mark Blackburn.

30 and 31. Æthelred's Long Cross penny. Photograph: Mark Blackburn.

32, 33, 34, 35. Coins issued by Swein Forkbeard. Photographs: Nationalmuseet, Copenhagen.

36 and 37. Coin issued by Olaf Tryggvason. Photographs: Nationalmuseet, Copenhagen.

38. The battle of Maldon described in the A-version of the Anglo-Saxon Chronicle. Reproduced by kind permission of the Master and Fellows of Corpus Christi College, Cambridge.

39. The C-version of the Anglo-Saxon Chronicle. By permission of the British Library.

Maps

Figures

Running Head Credit Lines

Chapter 1: Scene from a viking age picture stone from Stenkyrka, Gotland, Sweden. Courtesy of Jonathan Reeve JR915b39p473 700800.

Chapter 2: Nineteenth-century vision of a viking fleet, now supported by archeological discoveries. Courtesy of Jonathan Reeve JR918b39p653 700800.

Chapter 3: Scene from a viking age picture stone from Stenkyrka, Gotland, Sweden]. Courtesy of Jonathan Reeve JR916b39fp488b 700800.

Chapter 4: Drawing from the ninth-century Carolingian Utrecht

Cover Illustrations

Front cover illustrations: Scenes from a viking age picture stone from Stenkyrka, Gotland, Sweden. Courtesy of Jonathan Reeve JR915b39p473 700800 / JR916b39fp488b 700800

Index

TEMPUS – REVEALING HISTORY

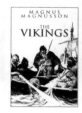

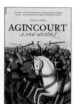

The Wars of the Roses
The Soldiers' Experience
ANTHONY GOODMAN
'Sheds light on the lot of the common soldier
as never before' *Alison Weir*
£25
0 7524 1784 3

The Vikings
MAGNUS MAGNUSSON
'Serious, engaging history'
BBC History Magazine
£9.99
0 7524 2699 0

William the Conqueror
DAVID BATES
'As expertly woven as the Bayeux Tapestry'
BBC History Magazine
£12.99
0 7524 2960 4

Agincourt: A New History
ANNE CURRY
'Overturns a host of assumptions about this
most famous of English victories... *the* book on
the battle' *Richard Holmes*
£25
0 7524 2828 4

Hereward The Last Englishman
PETER REX
'An enthralling work of historical detection'
Robert Lacey
£17.99
0 7524 3318 0

The English Resistance
The Underground War Against the Normans
PETER REX
'An invaluable rehabilitation of an ignored
resistance movement' **The Sunday Times**
£17.99
0 7524 2827 6

Richard III
MICHAEL HICKS
'A most important book by the greatest living
expert on Richard' *Desmond Seward*
£9.99
0 7524 2589 7

The Peasants' Revolt
England's Failed Revolution of 1381
ALASTAIR DUNN
'A stunningly good book... totally absorbing'
Melvyn Bragg
£9.99
0 7524 2965 5

If you are interested in purchasing other books published by Tempus, or in case you have difficulty finding
any Tempus books in your local bookshop, you can also place orders directly through our website:
www.tempus-publishing.com

 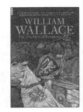

 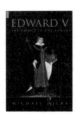